This book is a faithful copy of my notebook from the Grand Canyon river trip from Lee's Ferry to Diamond Creek. The editing is minimal, as I wanted to preserve my initial thoughts and reactions. Typed text was added three weeks after the trip, but it, too, is mostly unedited so that I could save my impressions before the memories of the trip faded

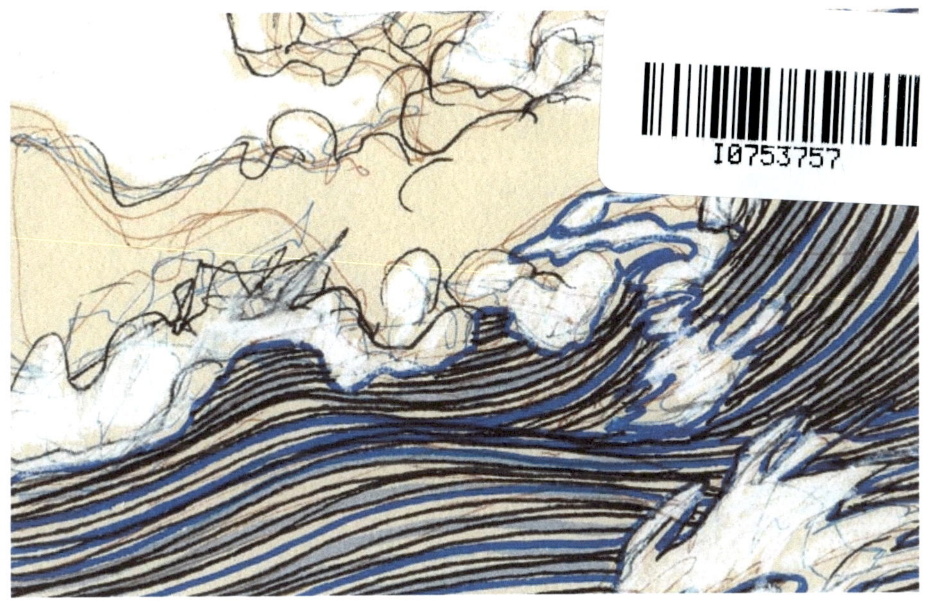

The first statement, on the inside cover of the original sketchbook, is a comment on scarce water. We were driving through the desert. It was dry, alkaline, and harsh. We were heading through a dry place to play in the water. I had the realization that we were about to play in a water supply for humans, the lifeblood of the desert, and a substance that is considered a right by many and a commodity by some.

Water
is
becoming
very
Scarce

[THE SURPLUS
IS GONE]

Grand Canyon Trip

Dec 19, 2010 Lee's Ferry
to to
Jan 2, 2011 Diamond Creek

"Be sure you pee in the river. Las Vegas (Lost Wages) needs all the water they can get." said the Ranger, during his safety lecture, just before we launched our trip.

So, exactly how much water is that wasteful city sucking from the only source in the desert???

The Colorado River

never reaches the ocean

A crack in the earth

One river, dammed in many places
is expected to provide life,
well beyond the most optimistic models,
even though it is already in severe
deficit; with much less water
coming into its watershed than
humans take out of it.

In the 1930s, the Colorado River
must be dammed to control floods
which destroyed foolish planning downstream
and give short term hope to the
~~those~~ people living in the desert.

Humans fool ourselves, so
our desires must be.

In the 1960s, the Colorado River
must be dammed to control floods
which made desperately needed water
run away from the desert farms,
even though dozens of models predicted
failure. Only the model that feeds our ego
must be.

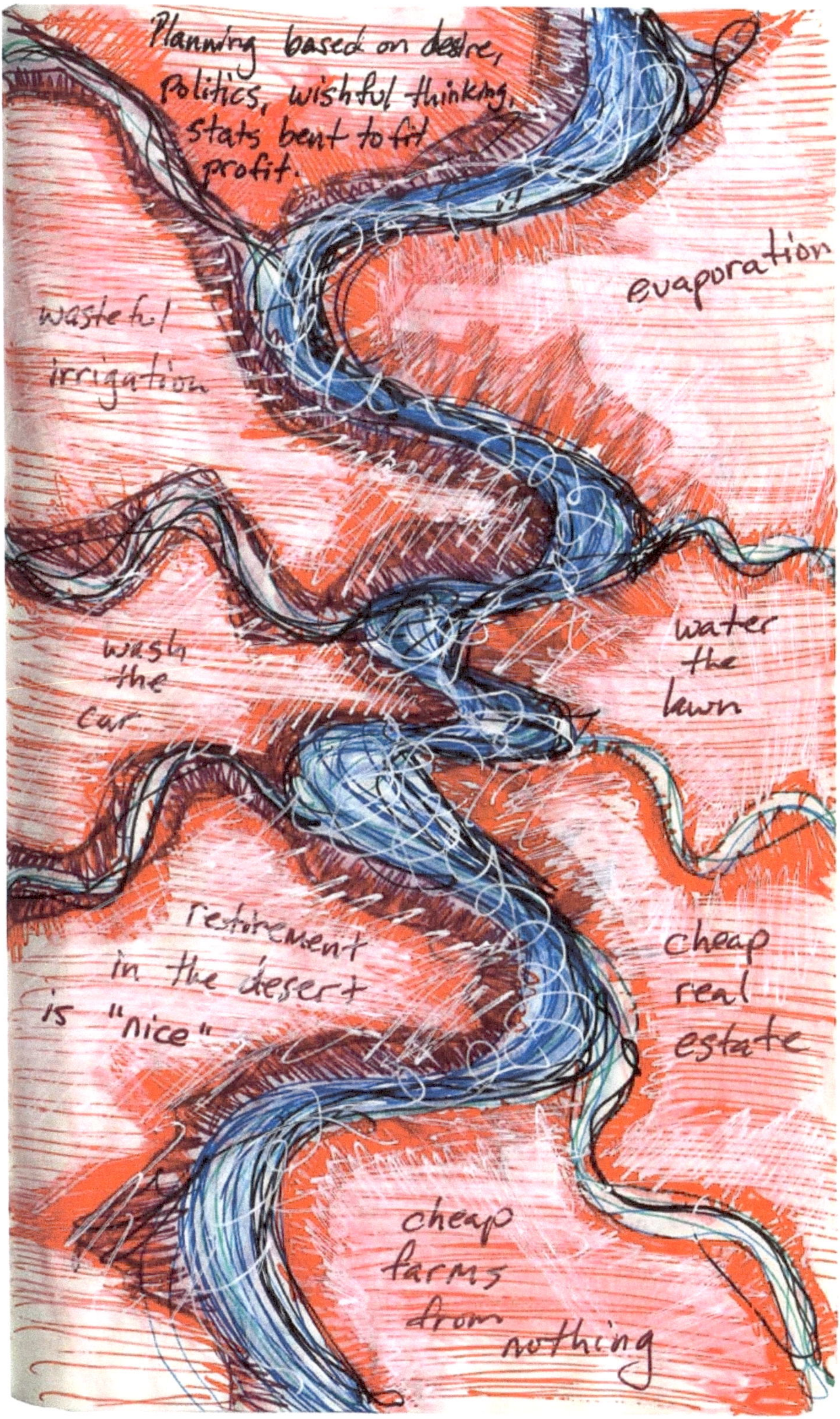

Planning based on desire,
politics, wishful thinking.
stats bent to fit
profit.

evaporation

wasteful
irrigation

wash
the
car

water
the
lawn

retirement
in the desert
is "nice"

cheap
real
estate

cheap
farms
from
nothing

We started in a desert, on December 19, 2010 at Lee's Ferry, with 3 rafts, loaded with too much food, several water cans, a good water filter, a mediochre first aid kit, 5 whitewater kayaks, some trepidation, 10 eager people, and a cursory understanding that the river is alive, and the desert that surrounds it is dry, fragile, harsh, and someplace we (humans) probably did not want to be, both for our sake, as well as for the sake of the fragile desert.

Our trip must be
on the river
and stay close to the river.

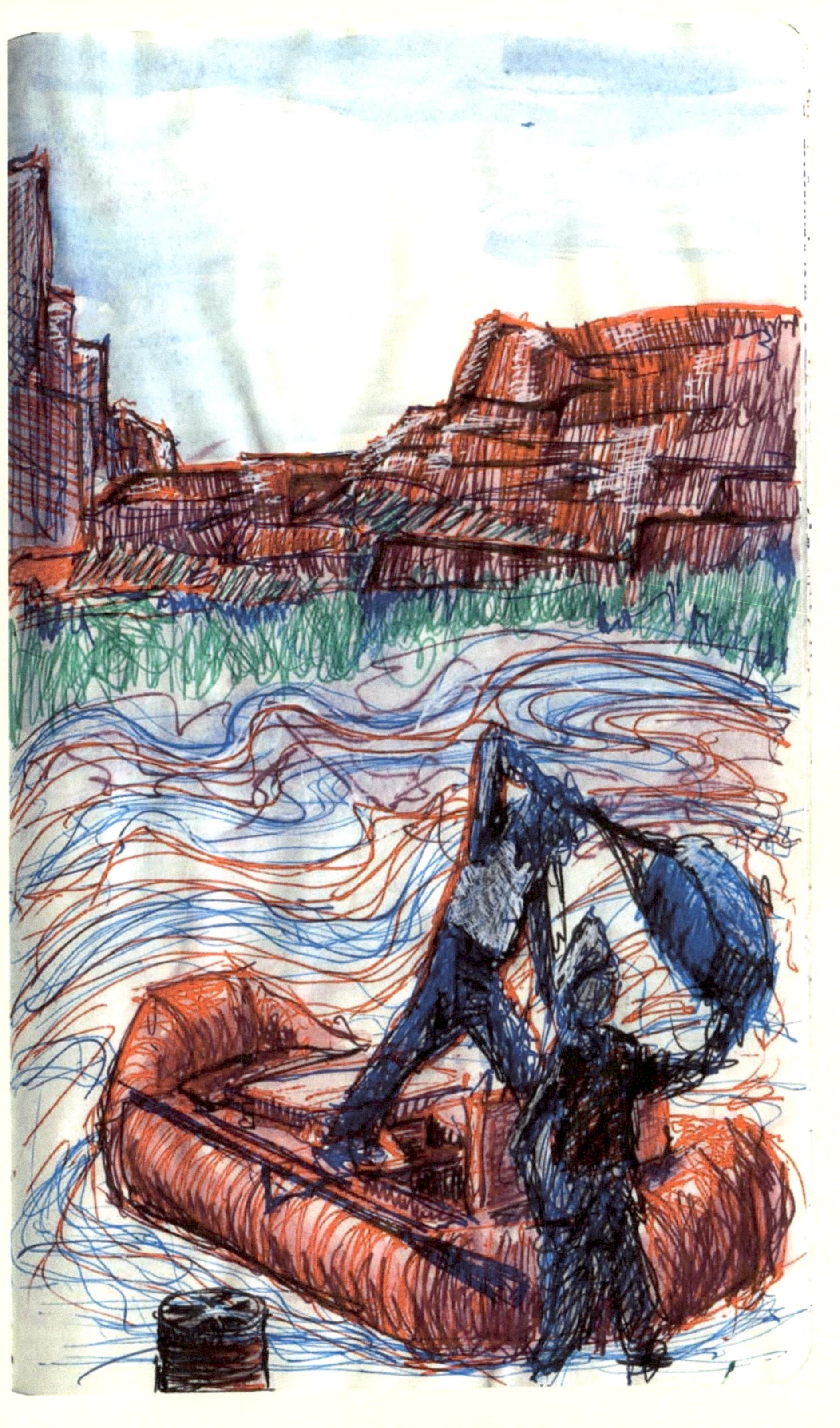

The water at the beginning of the Grand Canyon is blue-green. It is clear. The Glen Canyon dam is quickly filling with the natural sediment. Sediment fills Lake Powell as the still-water evaporates.

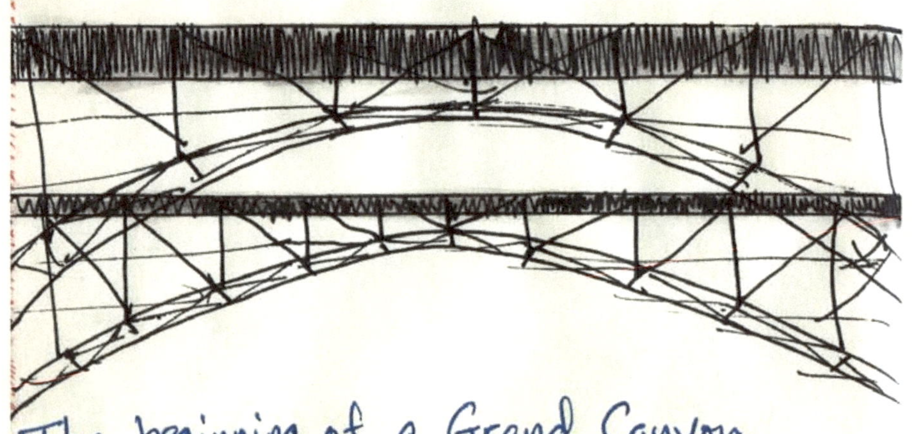

The beginning of a Grand Canyon river-trip is a tale of human impact. The upstream dam and shrinking lake. Un-naturally sediment-free water. A straight channel with few breaks. The steel Navaho Bridge at river mile 4½. Not until Ten Mile Rock does the Grand Canyon begin to feel like the spectacle of nature it is.

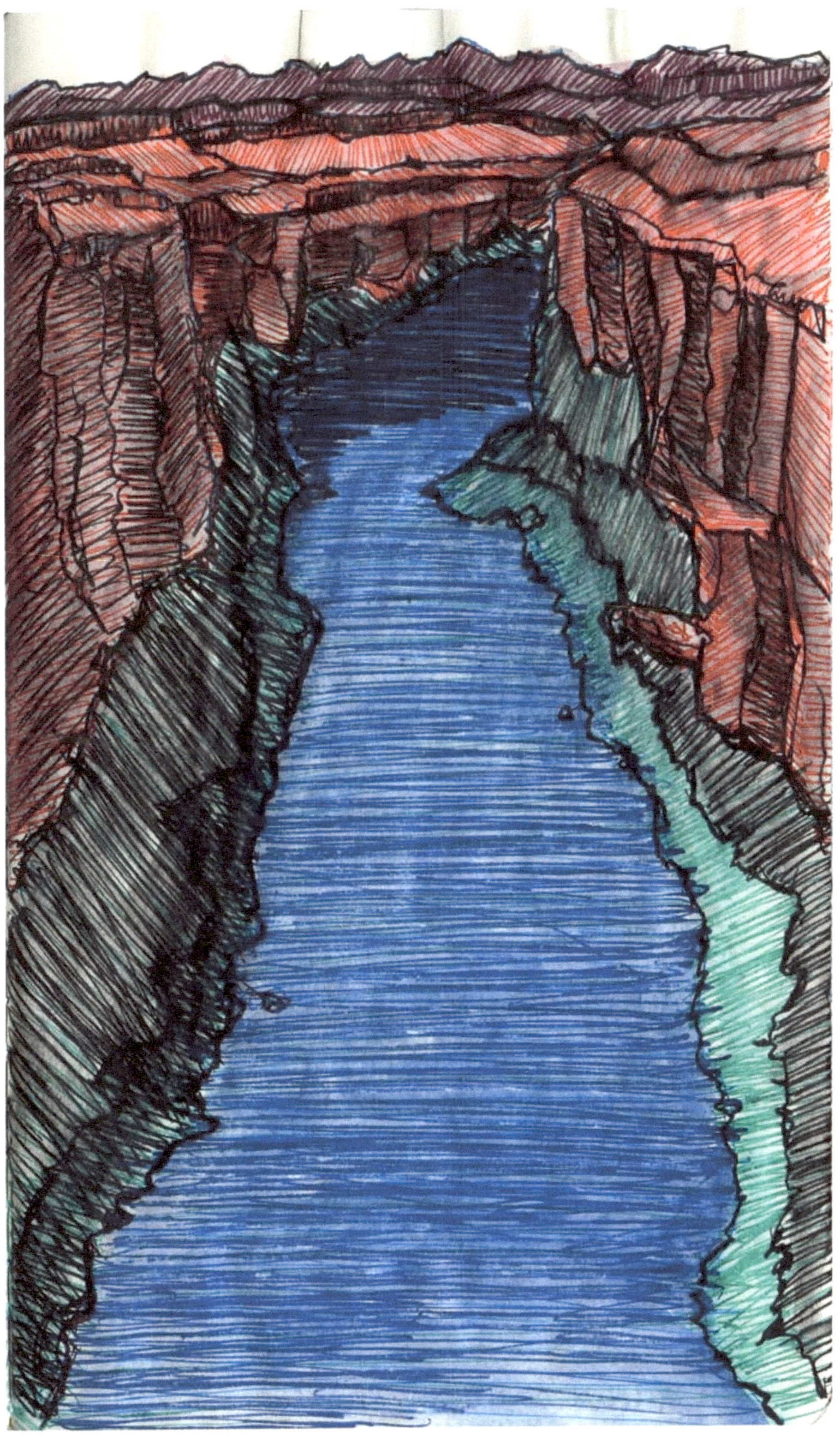

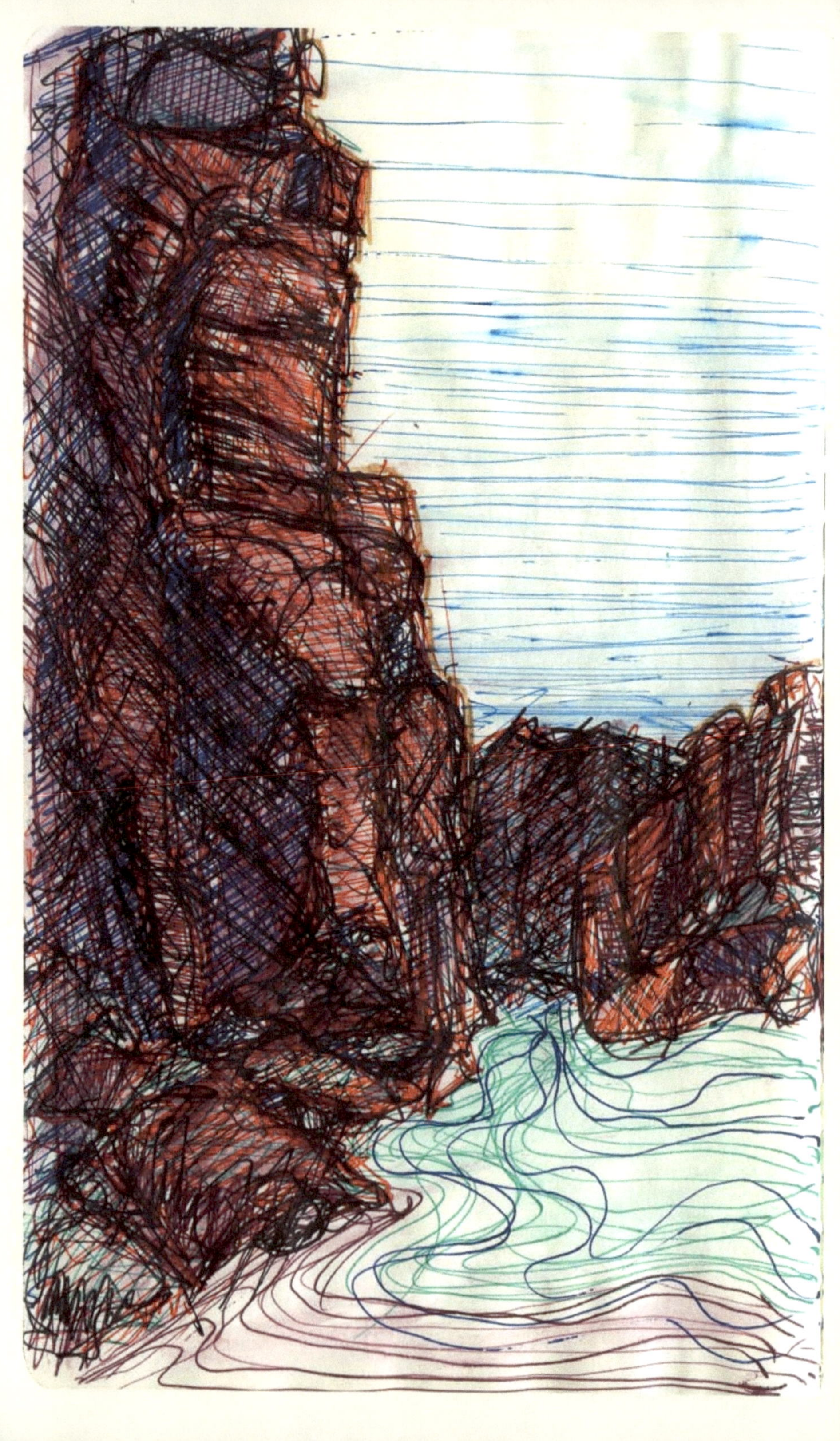

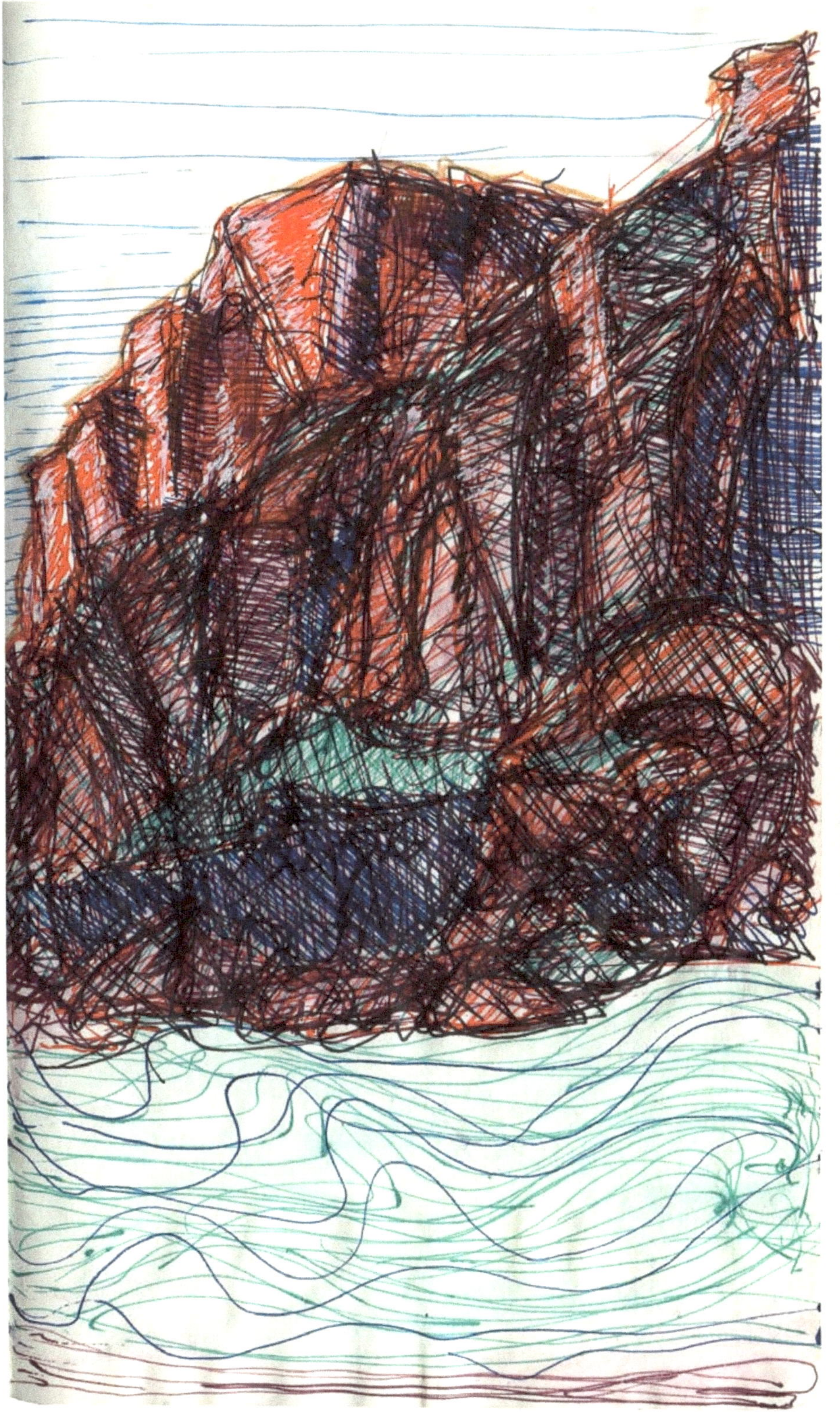

The Grand Canyon is an entropic system of erosion, with the Colorado River being both agent of chaos and order. It saws deep slots in the most durable rock. The river provides life along its banks, turning thin boundaries to lush green that contrast with the pervasive red limestone and black basalt. The river is an oasis in an otherwise sandy, dry, extreme desert environment.

Animals most live within a short distance of the Colorado, or one of the tributaries. Life is most abundant along the banks. Scorpions find more shelter from the burning sun, within the canyon walls. Mice thrive on organic material and humans' food along the river. More mice means more rattlesnakes. Ravens follow people down the Colorado, and poach unattended treats. Herons and condors patrol the ribbon of life for food and water.

The tidal fluctuation of the river ties all life along its corridor. Humans control the ebb and flow with a giant dam. But, models that predict the inflow behind Glen Canyon dam are guesswork. We cannot control what we don't know.

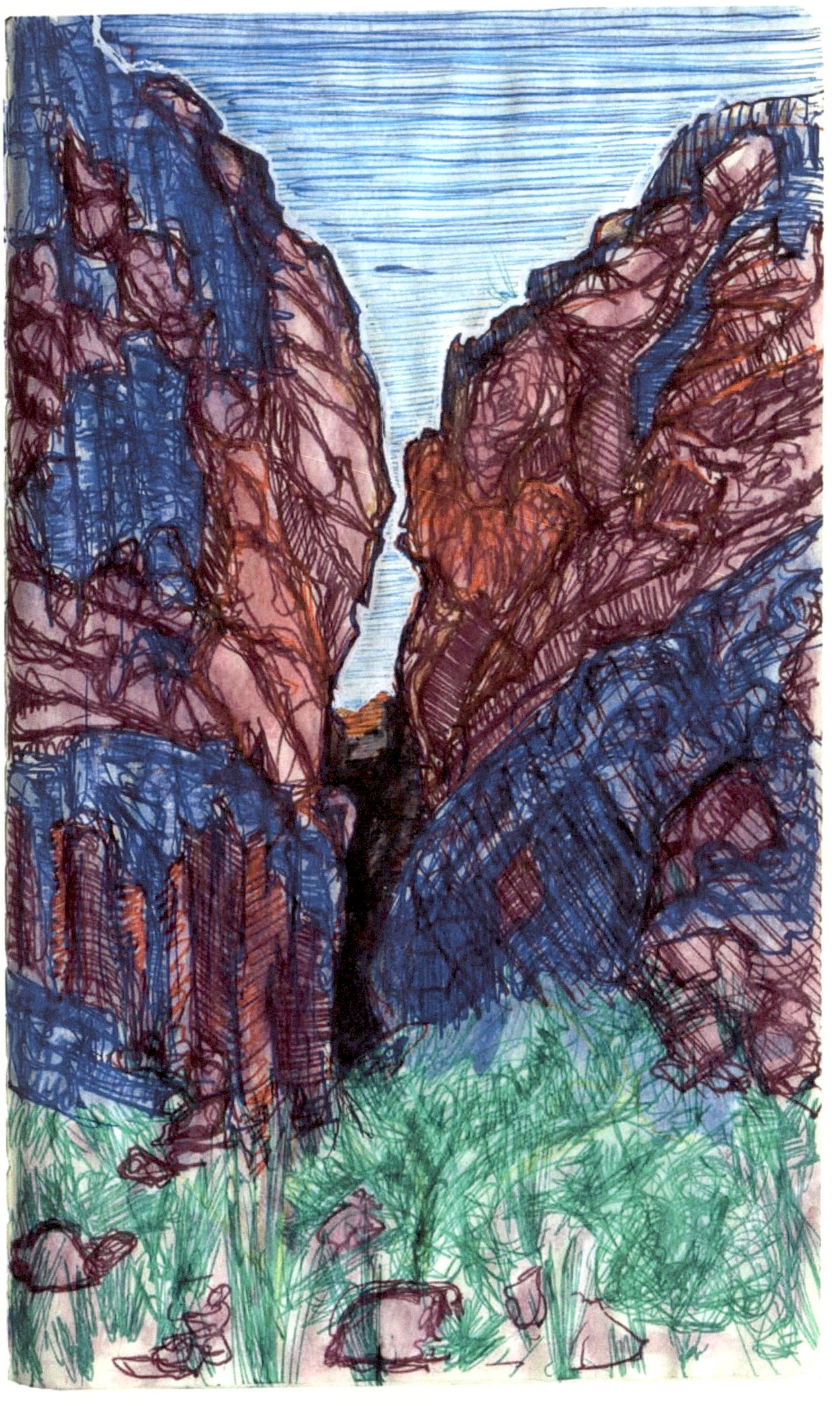

Pathfinding through a rapid is a special skill. Boatmen learn to use the water to help them dance around some of the dangerouse features. Sometimes, however, you cannot avoid the breaking wave (or hole) and it must be run head on, squared up, and right down the middle. (Hey diddle diddle...)

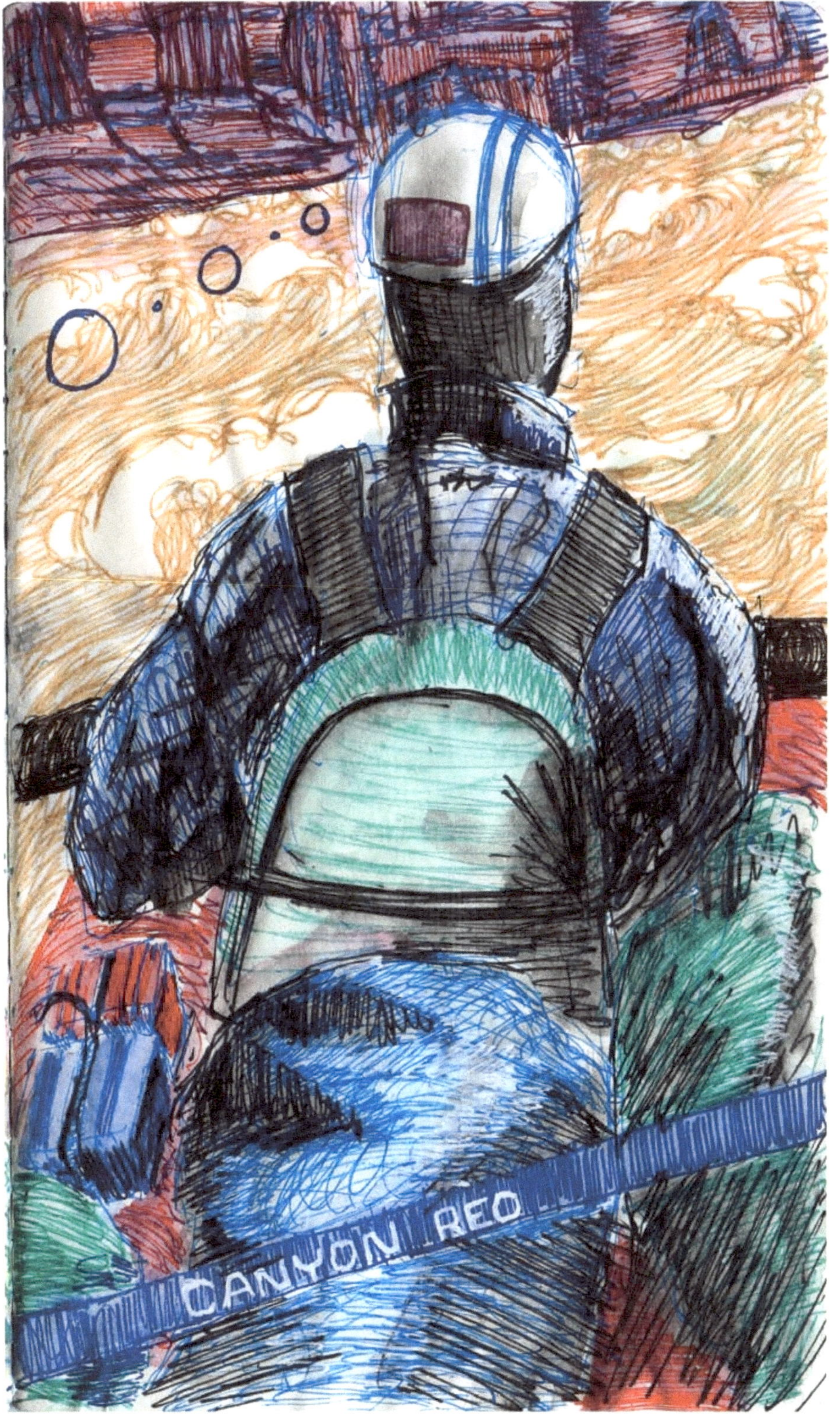
CANYON REO

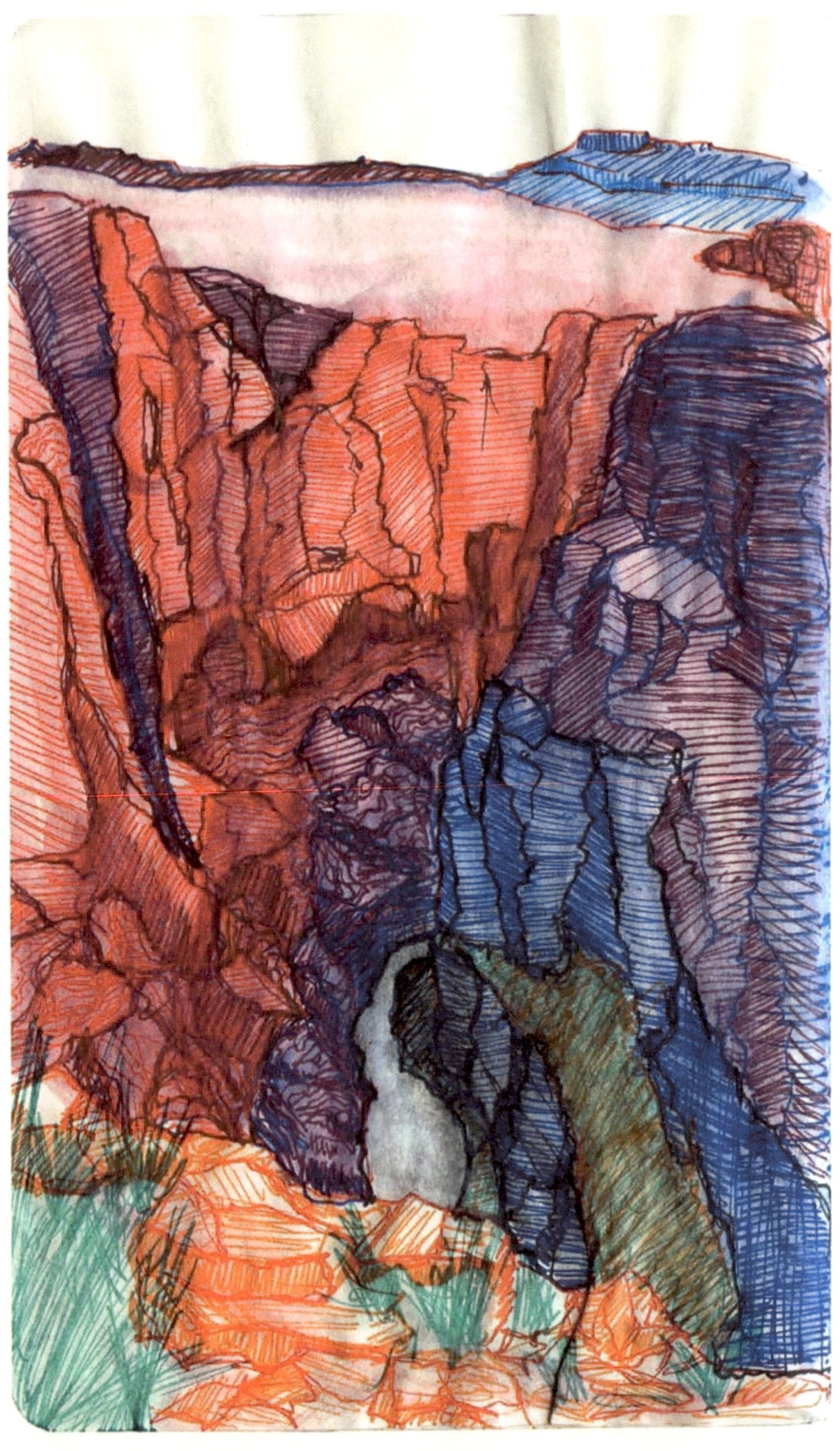

The Little Colorado River joins the main stem of the Colorado River at mile 62. Turquoise water flows from what some believe is a sacred site to Hopi Indians. Today, Navaho see the Little Colorado as a life-giving part of their evolution tales.

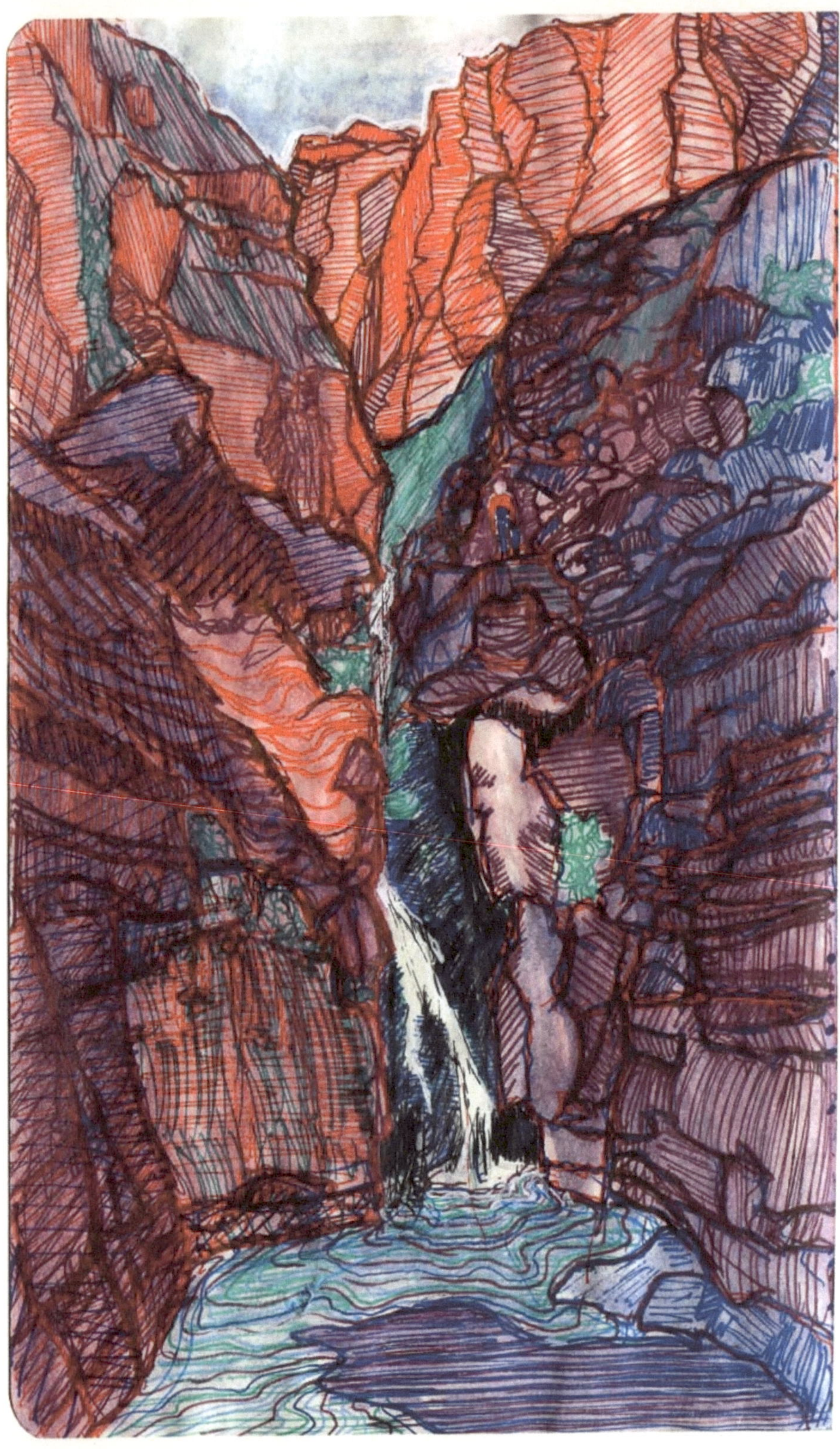

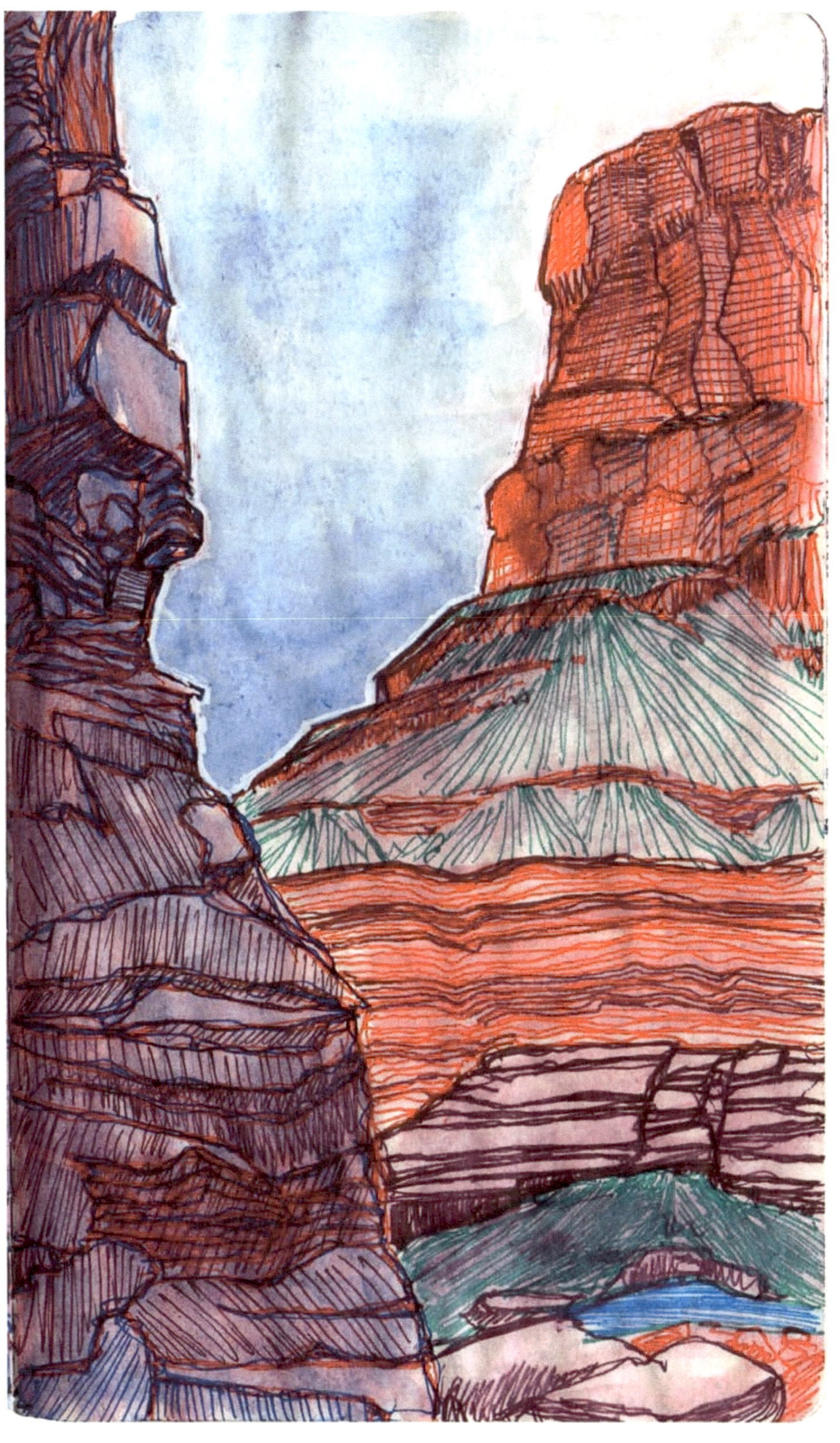

Camp site at mile 118.6, not far from Elves Chasm, has evidence of high water (about 20 feet above current flows) in the carved limestone walls, with small overhanging cliffs and striated face up to the high water mark. Horizontal lines contrast the vertical thrust of the upper layers of stone, in a part of the Grand Canyon that reaches nearly one mile high.

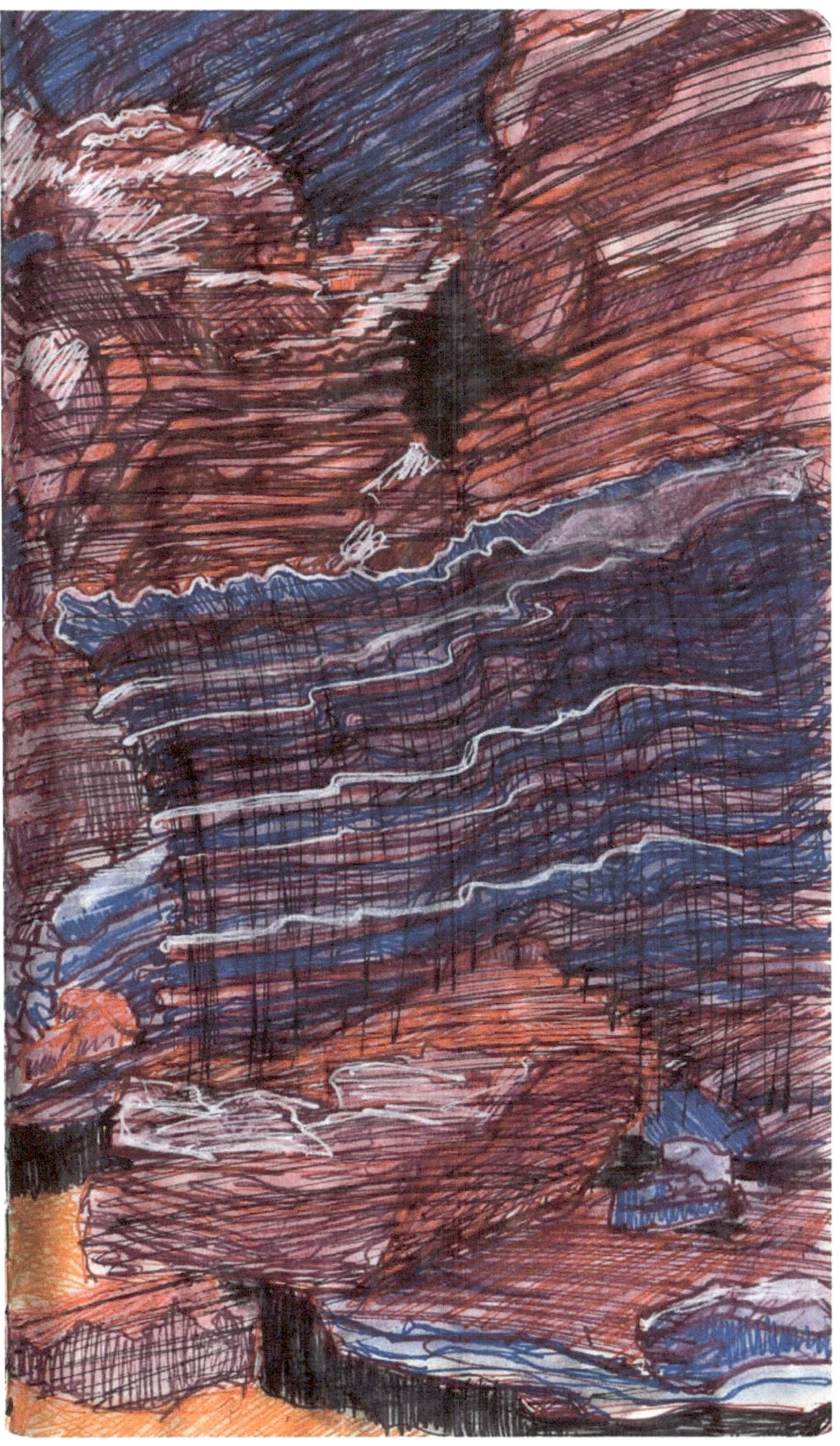

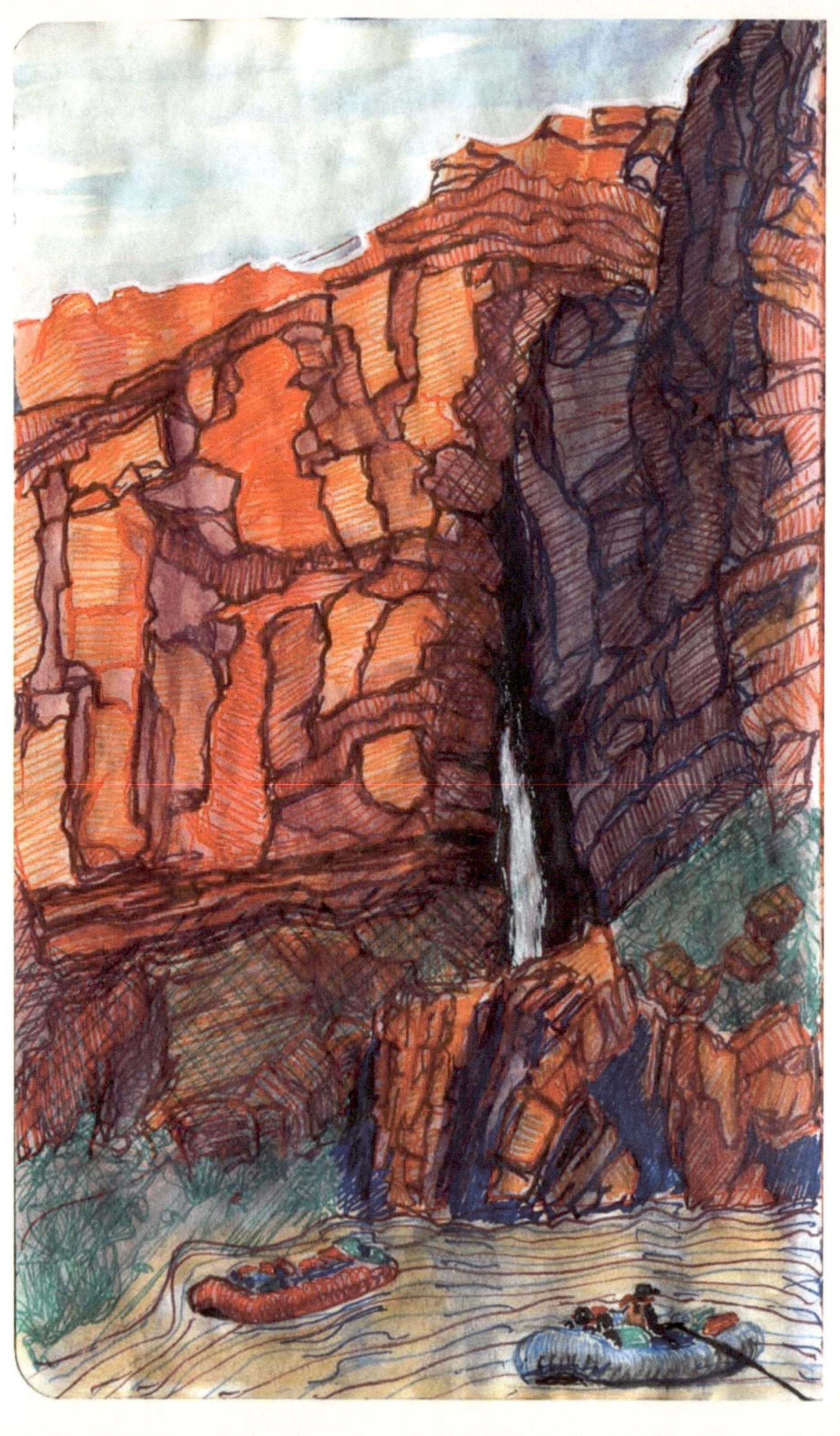

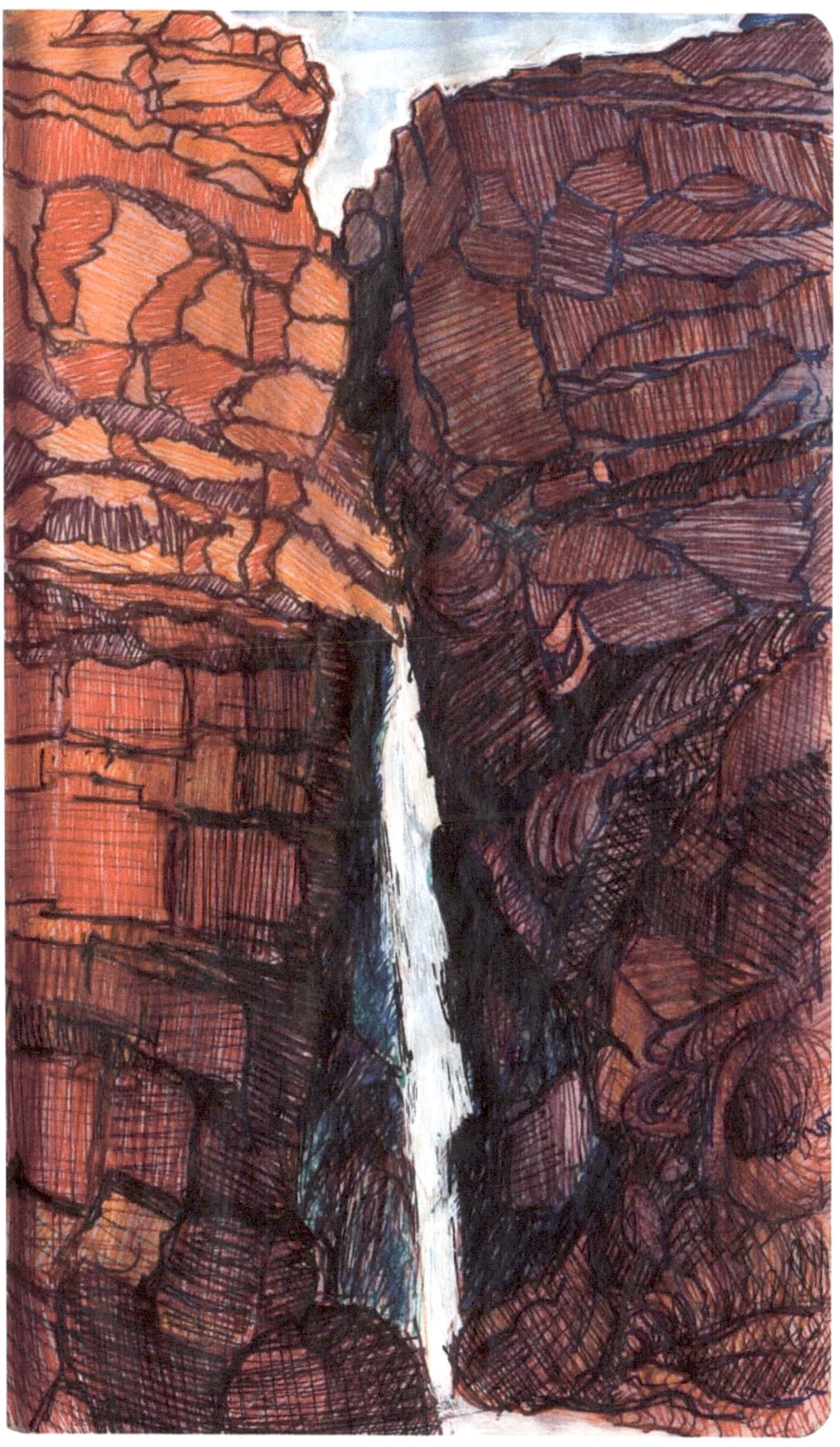

We spent the night across the river from Deer Creek Falls. The next morning, after breakfast, most of the crew hiked up the side to explore the creek itself, which cut a narrow canyon until it pushes through the rock and falls down the cliff face to meet with the Colorado.

In the middle of the trip, we navigated some rapids that, had any of them been on a single-day trip, would have been of slightly less concern. There is, of course, always a risk, but since we were carrying all of our gear for a 15 day trip, with no way out except a helicopter, we had to treat each wave with more respect. Often, the most conservative line was to ride a line on top of an angled wave, reactionary wave, or turbulent eddy line so that we could avoid the deepest parts of a wave/ hole while not getting caught by one of the hundreds of strong eddies. It is called "riding the dragon's back" because although it is a wild ride, you are getting out of the teeth of the rapid.

The downstream reward (in addition to the thrill of riding the dragon's back) was the abundance of fun side hikes through small canyons cut by tributaries of the Colorado River. Matkatamiba and Havasu Canyon are within 10 miles of each other and were highlights of the trip.

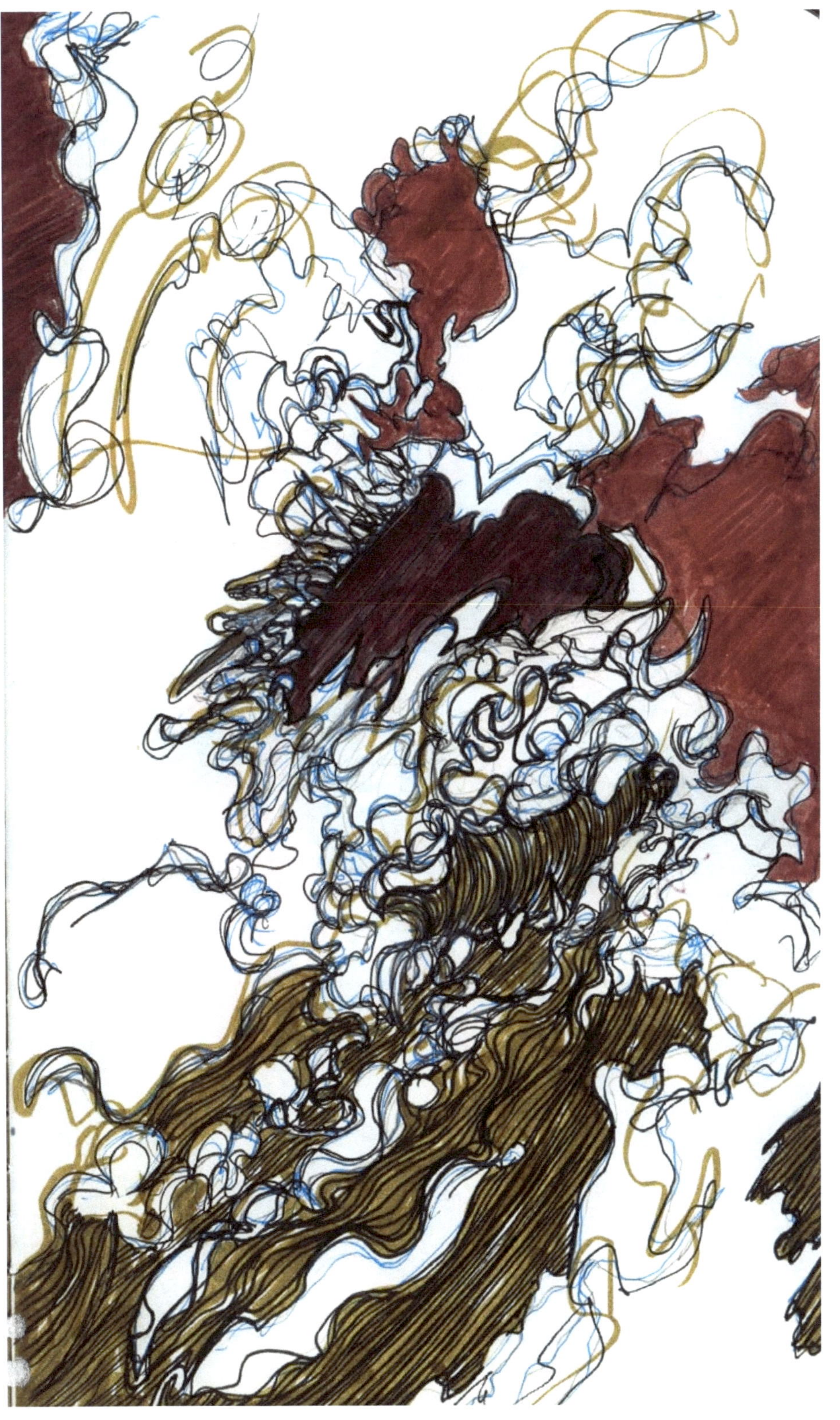

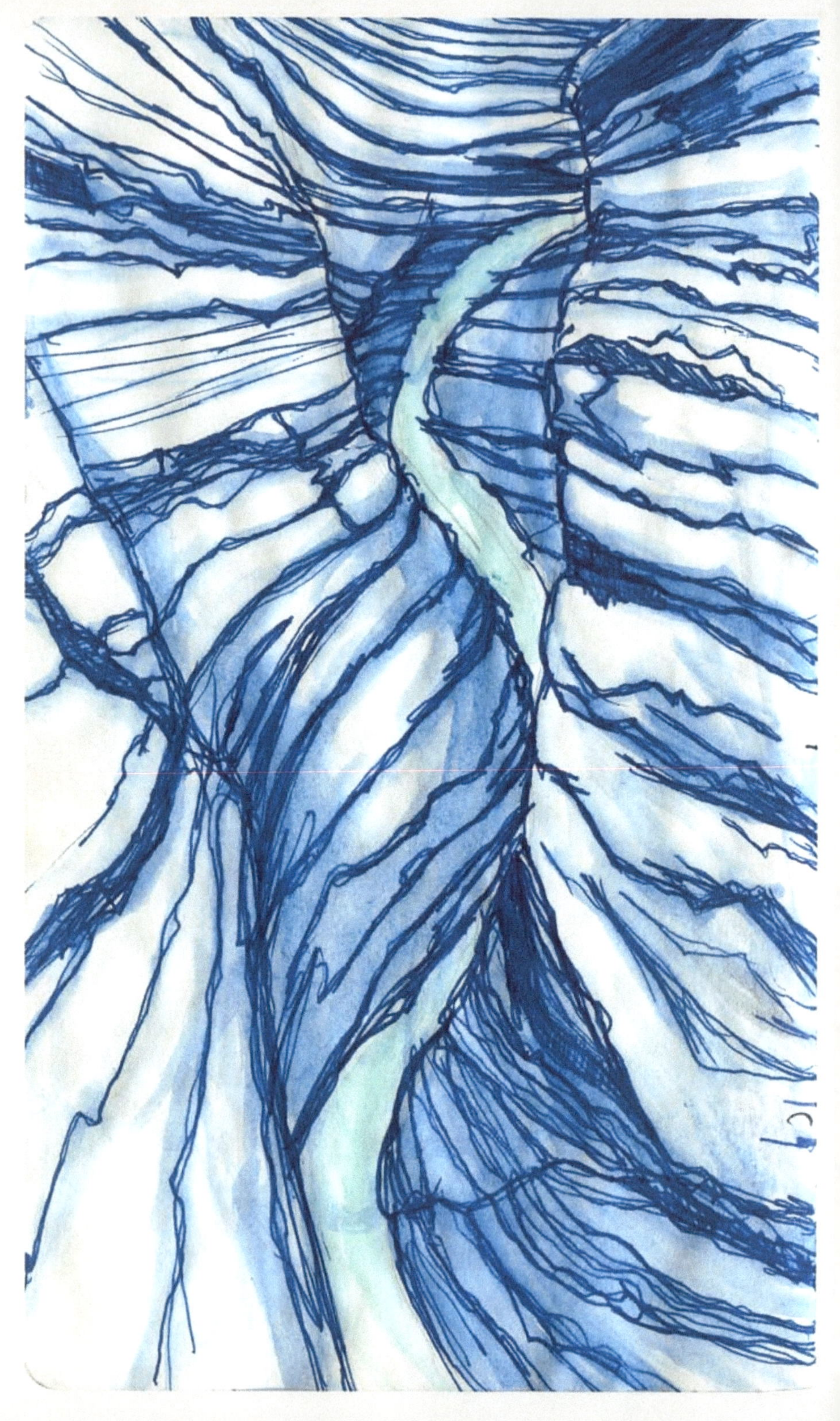

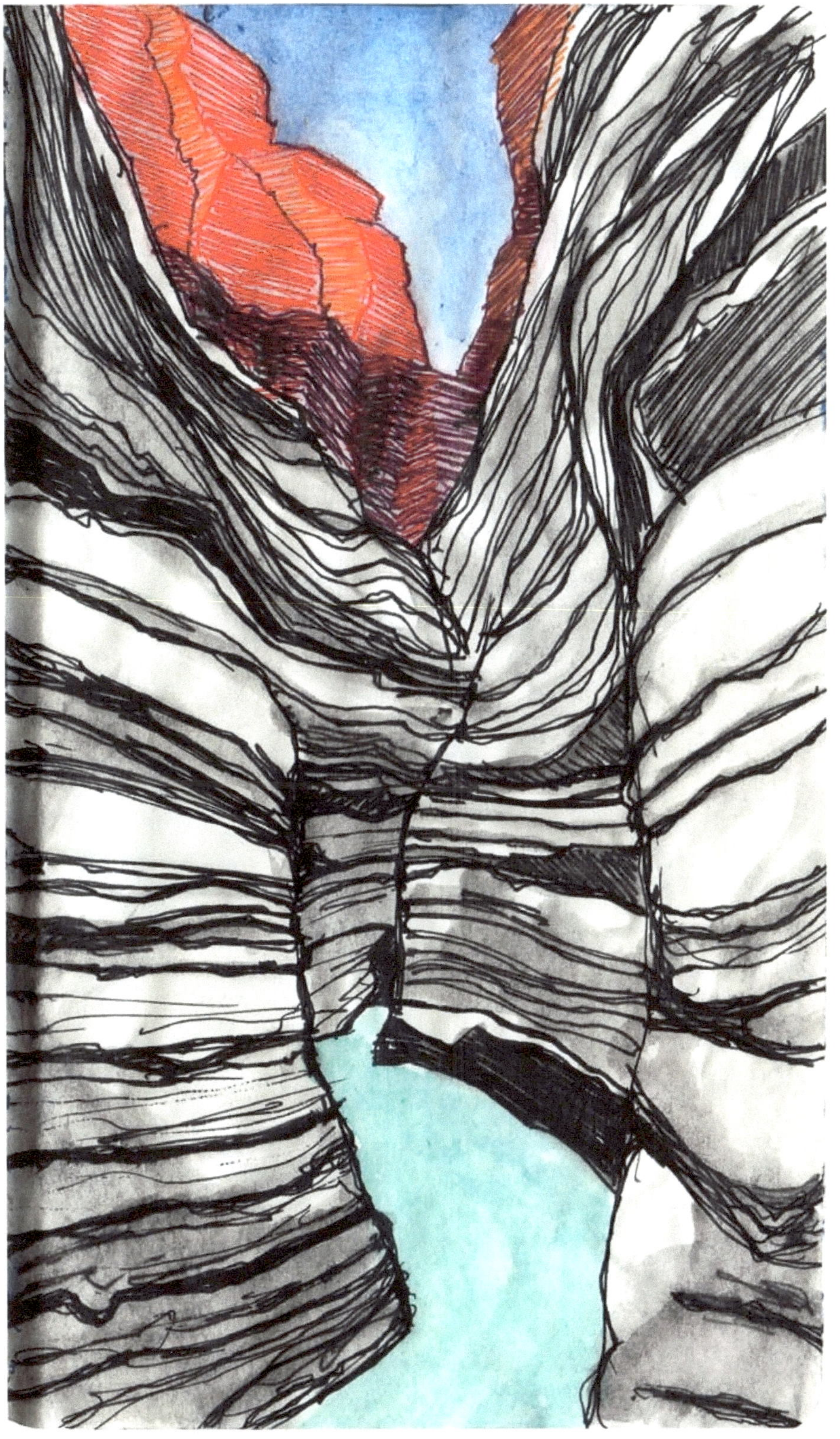

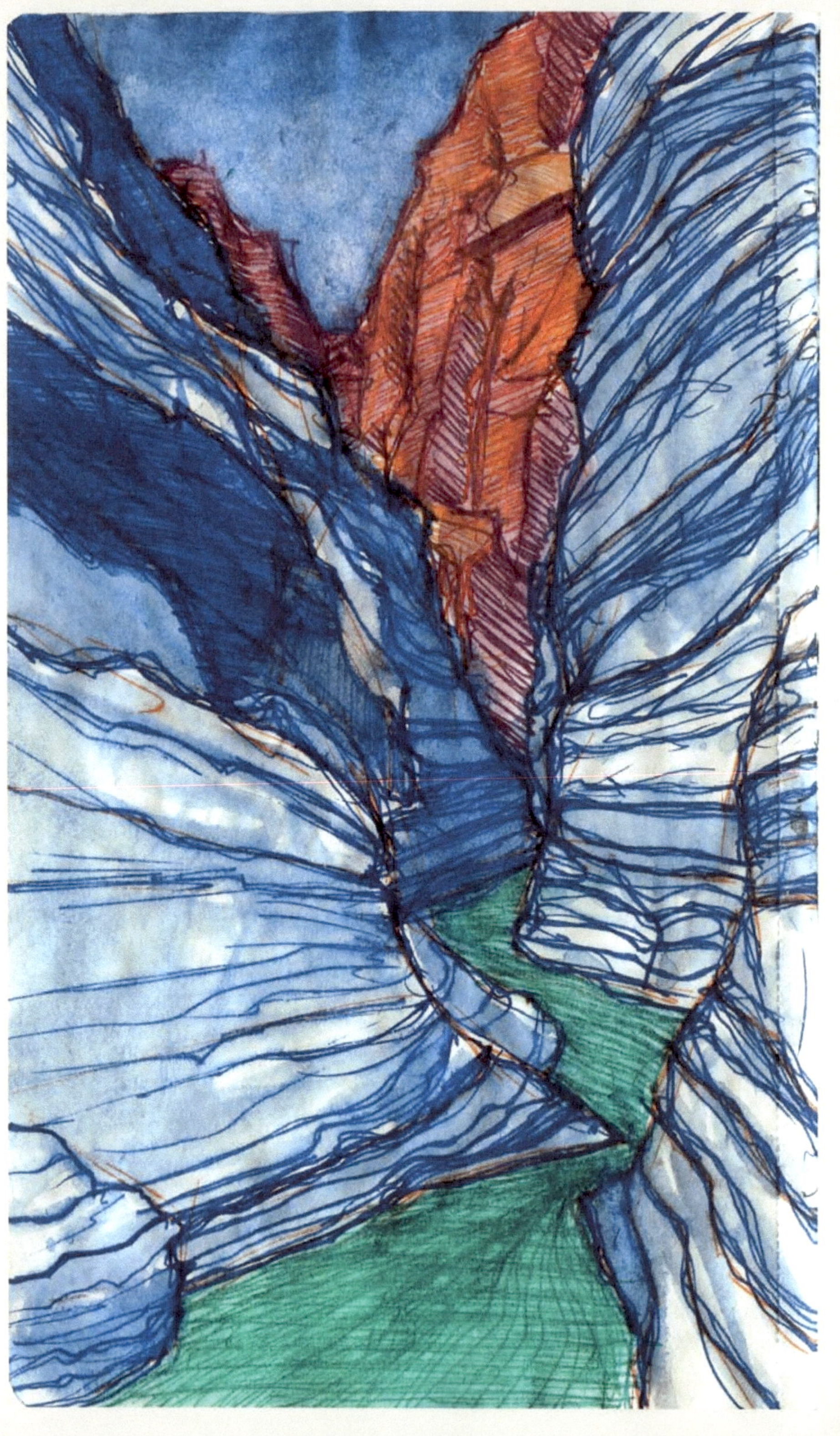

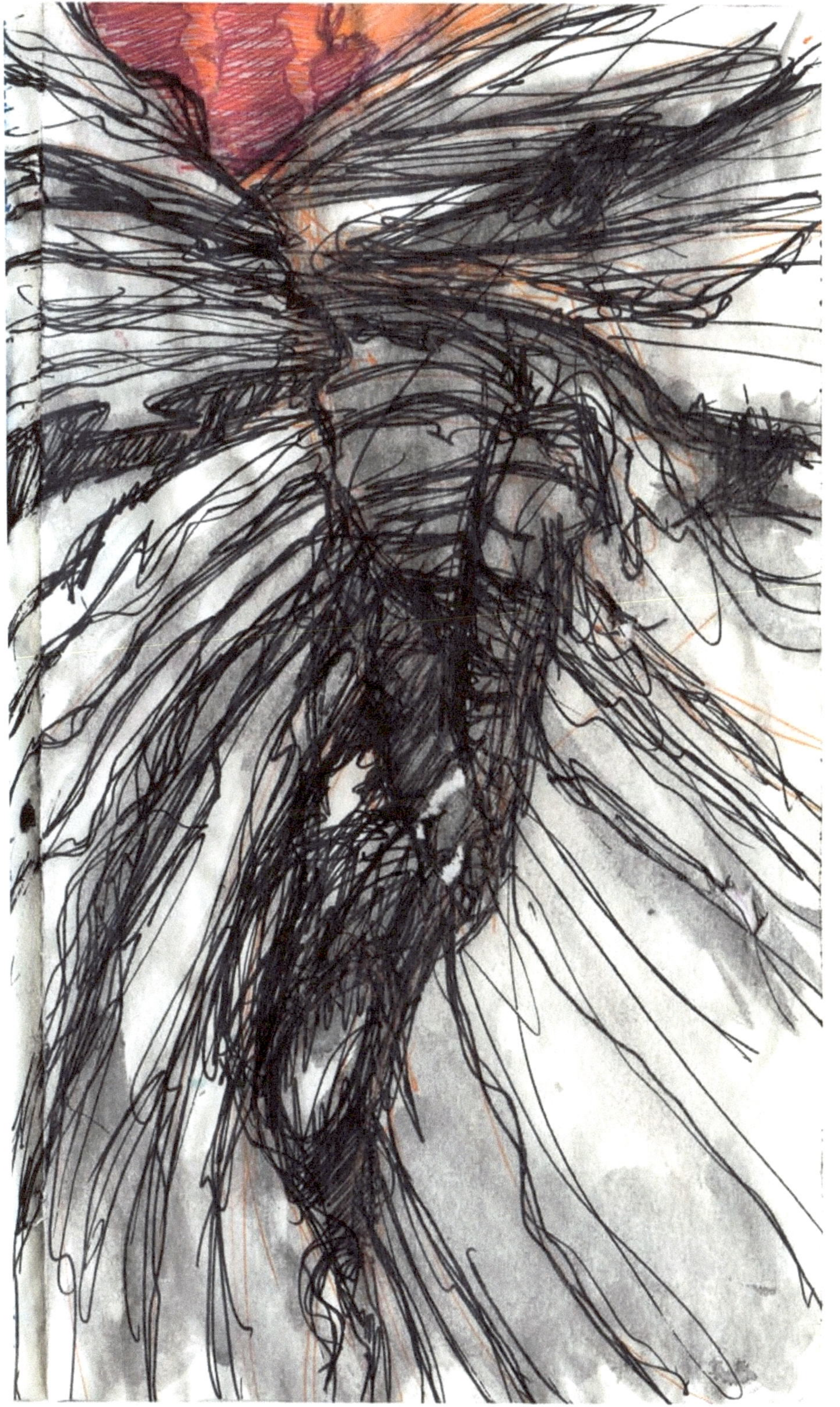

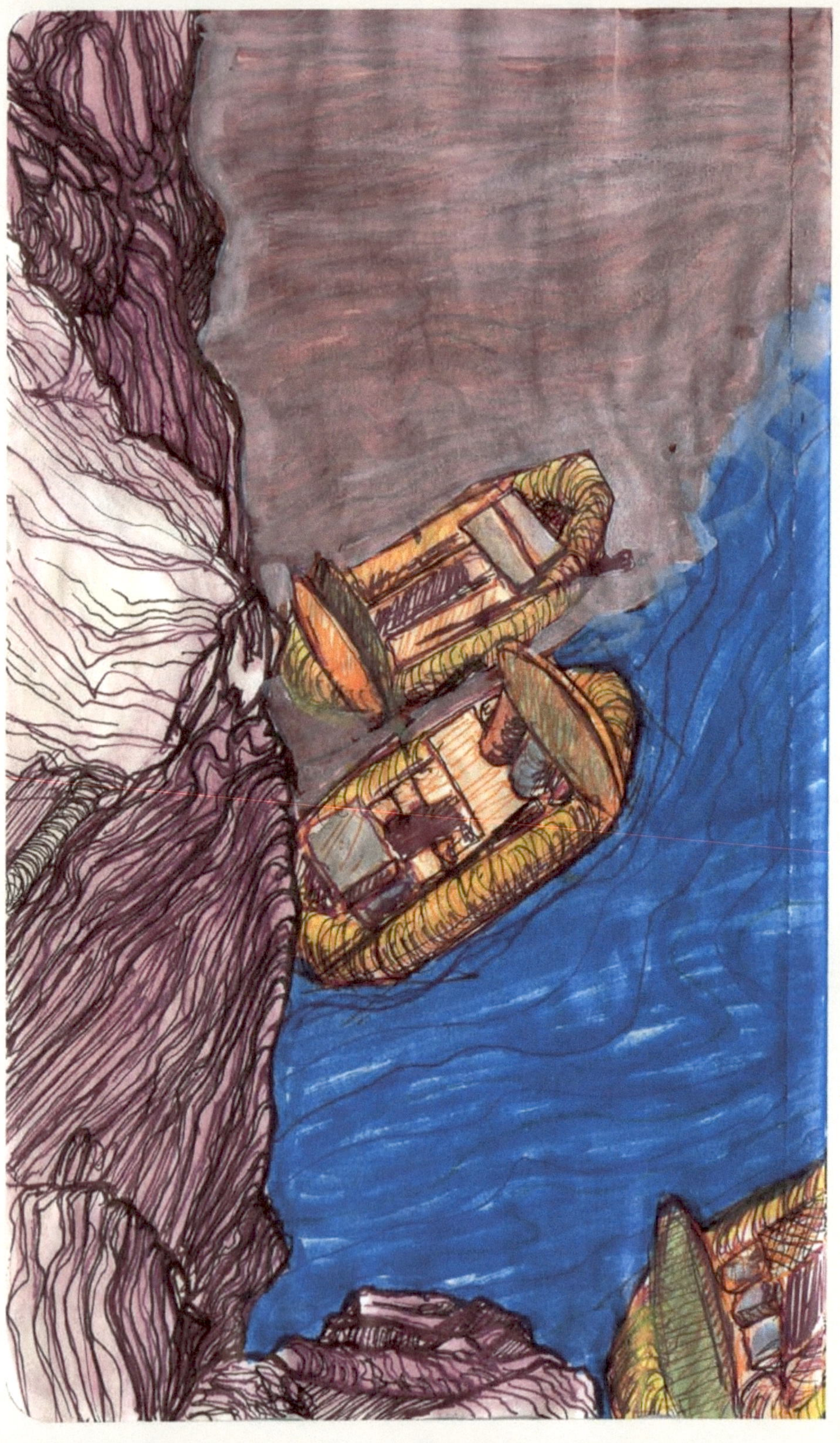

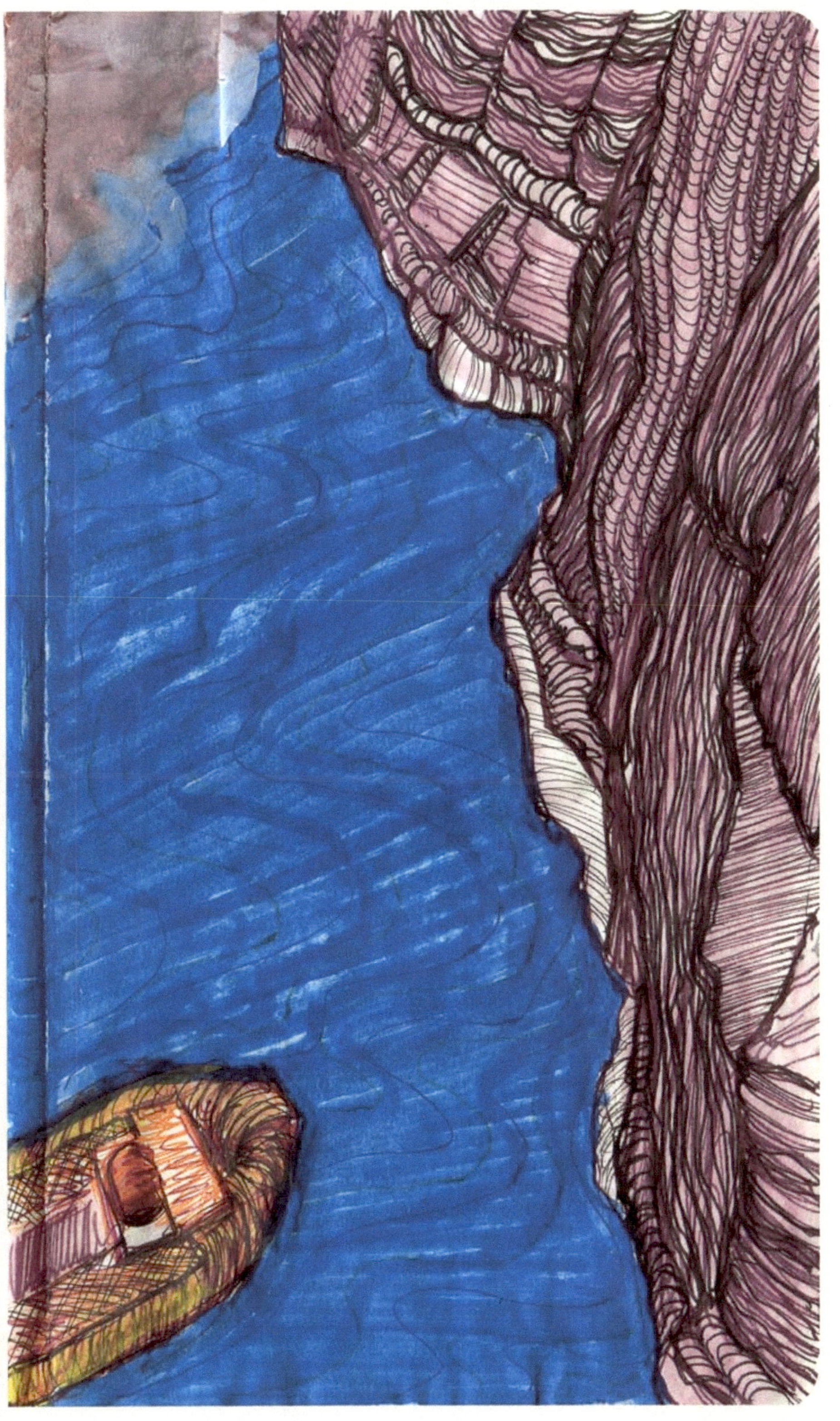

Black basalt dams were created by lava flows (a very long time ago) large enough to block the river and create a lake several times larger than Lake Powell. This igneous rock eventually gave way to the insistence of the Colorado River and let the massive lake drain. Remnants of the massive dam, created from durable stone, born from inside the earth's mantle, can be seen often below Mile 179 on a Grand Canyon river trip. Old flows meet the river. Some continue on the other side, revealing an ancient breach in a basalt dam.

The river must be allowed to flow. If it can break durable basalt, made by the earth itself, then what makes us think it will not, one day, remove all human-made structures?

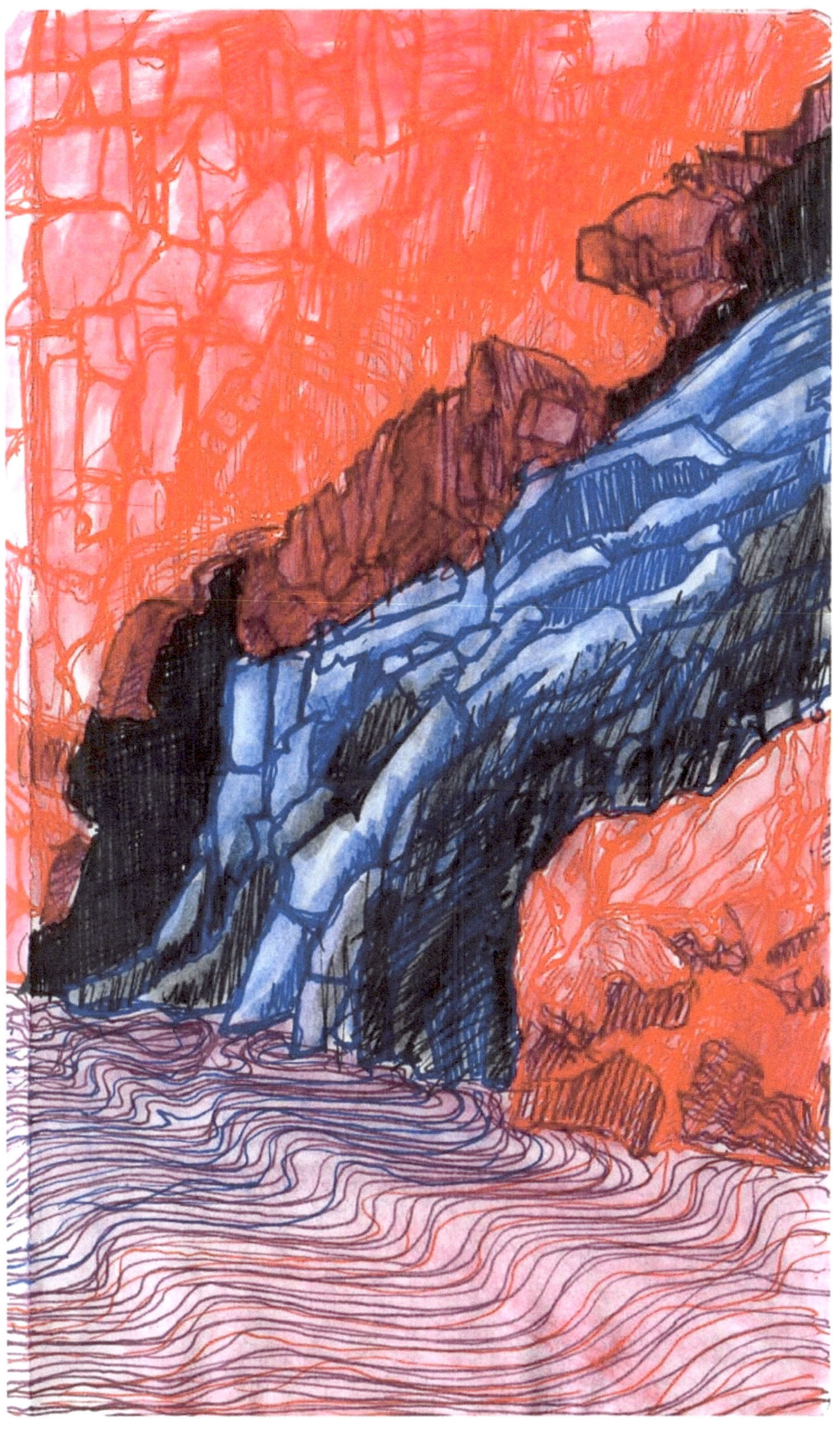

Camped across from Vulcan's Anvil, the gray sky and cold weather pulled color from the valley as we tried to stay warm. Clothes hung around the fire pan, while dinner cooked and everyone set up camp at a terrific site. Thoughts still turned to the next day's rapid, the one rated with the highest difficulty.

Lava Falls is not a technically difficult rapid. The main move is to avoid the giant hole at the top, then take the hit from all the waves in the rest of it. But, Lava has been known to force 18 foot rafts under water while magic fingers pull loose equipment into the surrounding water.

The rain was mild until we were finished with dinner, and most of our gear was dry. The wind picked up throughout the night, knocking the make-shift kitchen tent down at 2 am. I woke, disoriented, to the sound of high wind and people's voices in the background. Emerging from my tent disoriented, I found most of the crew folding the tarp around the kitchen, and adding gear bags to the corners for weight. We all went back to our sleeping bags to get as much rest as the cold night and wind would allow. Tomorrow was a big day.

Lava Falls is created by the combination of an ancient dam from the volcano called Vulcan's Throne and debris from floods in Prospect Canyon. I had a plan. So, I thought....

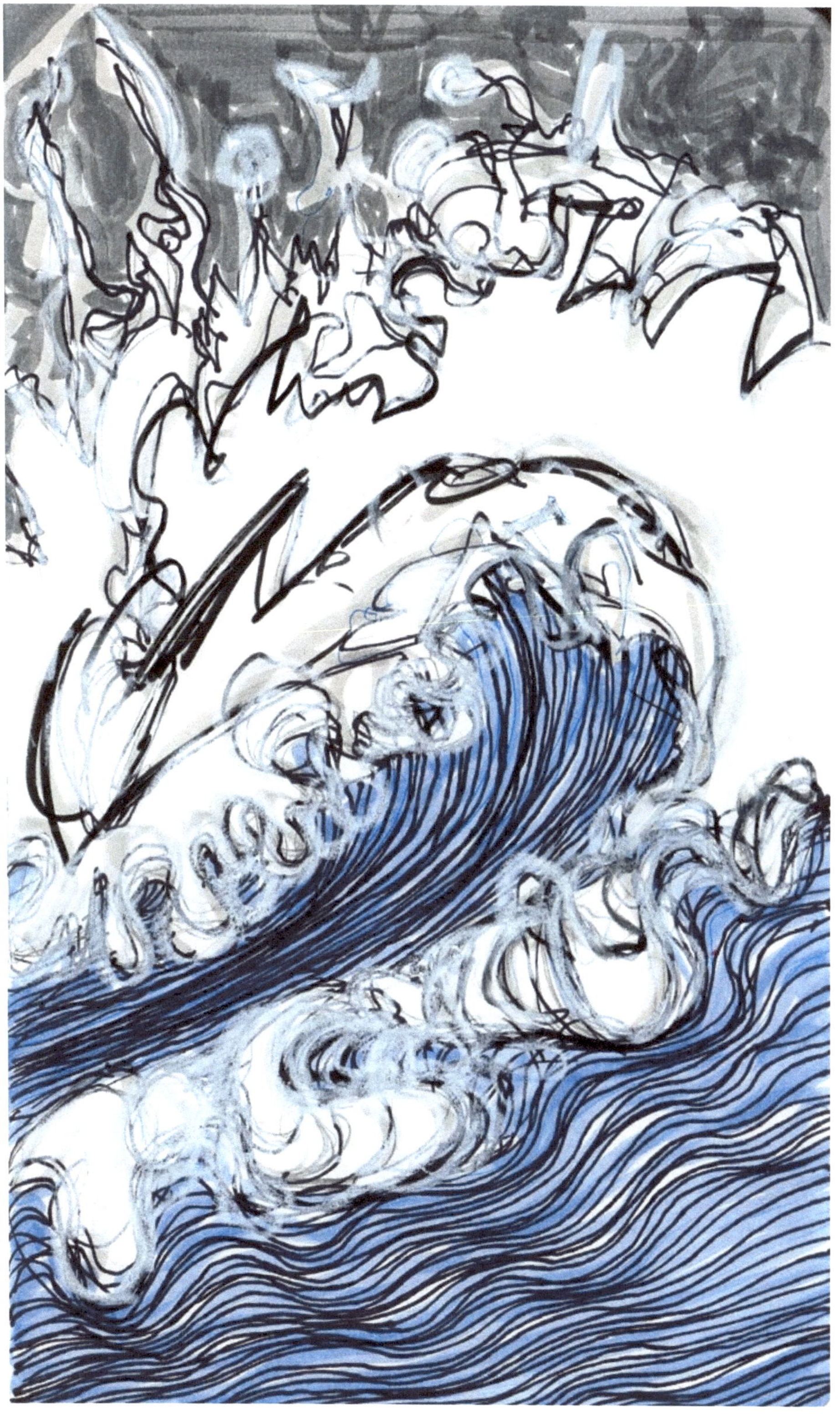

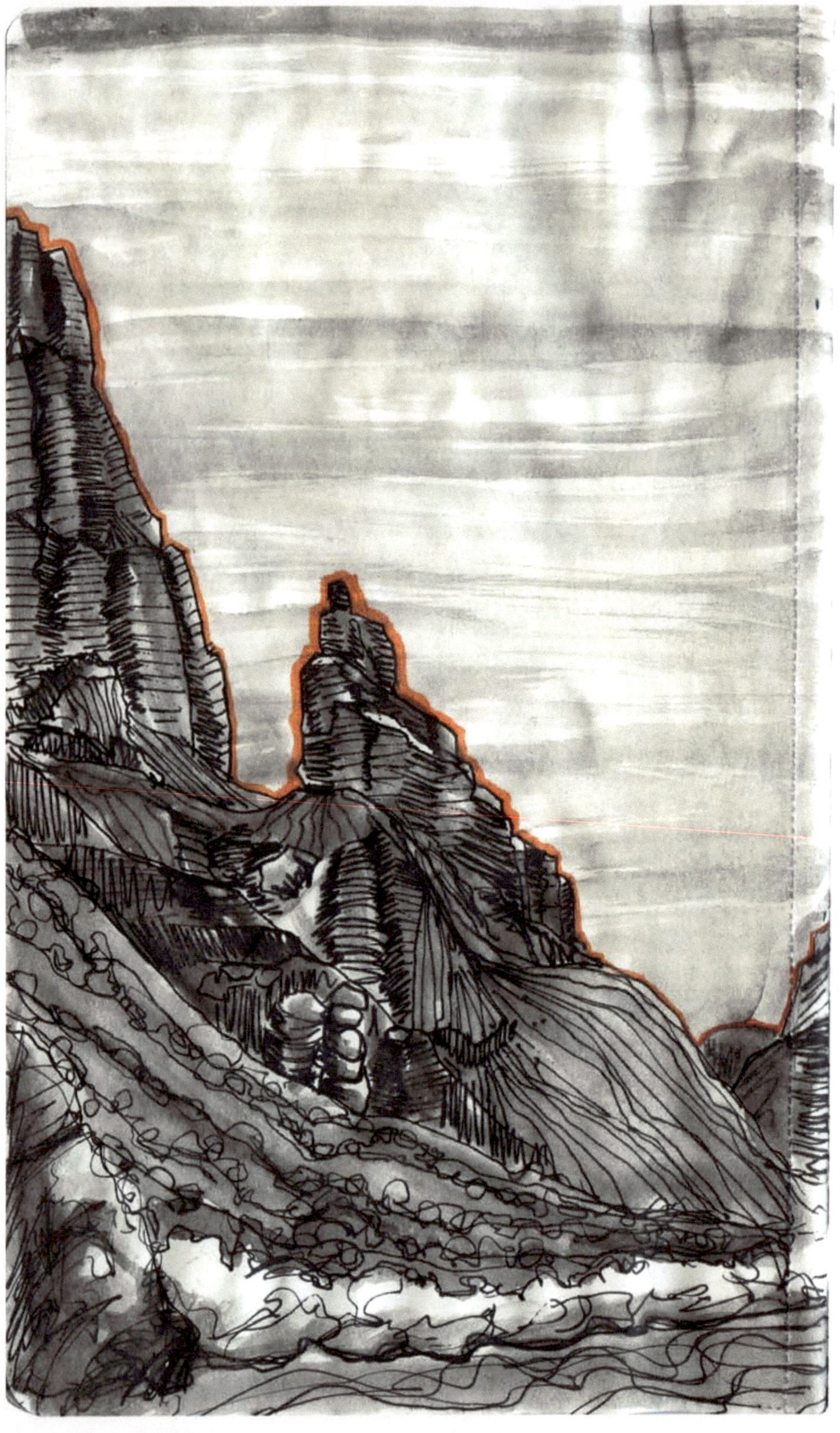

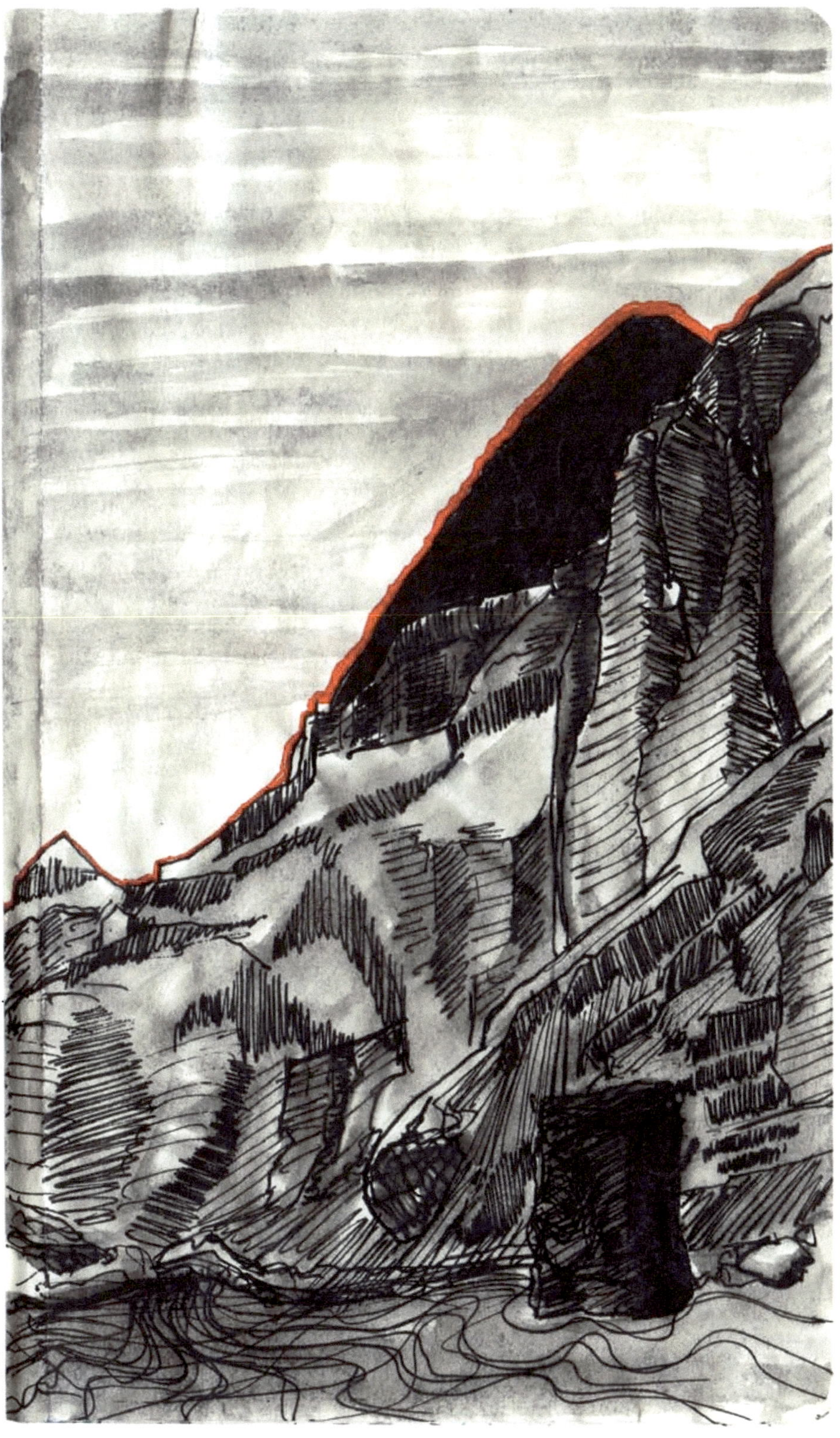

I RODE THE EDDY LINE ON THE RIGHT, THEN PADDLED HARD TO THE LEFT WHEN I THOUGHT I WAS NEAR THE GIANT HOLE IN THE CENTER. MY MOVE TO THE LEFT WAS TOO EARLY. IT WAS LATE ENOUGH TO AVOID THE HOLE, BUT EARLY ENOUGH TO BITE OFF TOO MUCH OF THE CRASHING WAVE. THE WAVE WAS SURGING AND CRASHING, SO I MIGHT HAVE HAD AN UNLUCKY MOMENT AND MET IT JUST AS IT CRASHED. I MIGHT HAVE BEEN TOO FAR LEFT. WHATEVER THE REASON WAS, I DID END UP KNOCKED BACK TO THE RIGHT, SIDEWAYS, AND HAD TO SCRAMBLE TO GET THE BOAT POINTED DOWNSTREAM IN TIME TO HIT THE "V" WAVE. I WENT UNDERWATER, AND ACCORDING TO EVERYONE WATCHING, TRAVELLED AT LEAST 15' BEFORE REAPPEARING LIKE A TRIDENT MISSILE, SUPPORTED BY ONLY THE LAST 6 INCHES OF MY STERN. FORTUNATELY, I WAS SQUARE IN MY BOAT AND LANDED FLAT, ALLOWING ME TO FINISH THE REST OF THE RAPID ON LINE.

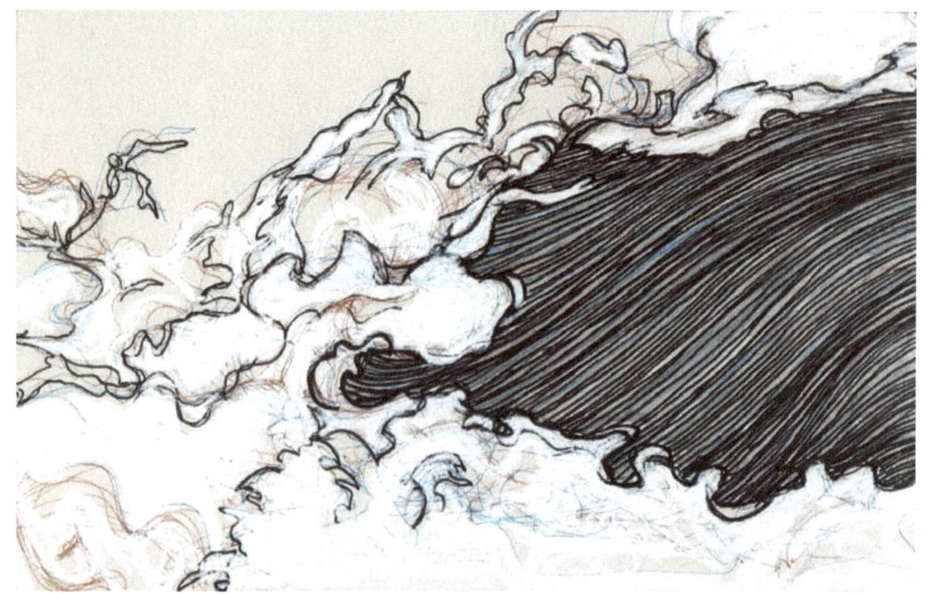

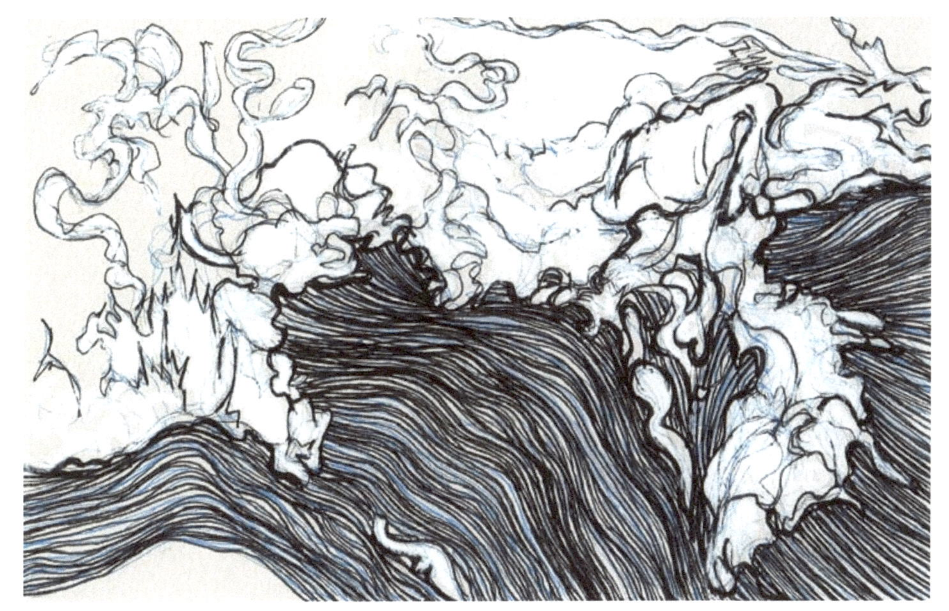

The rest of the crew chose much more straight forward lines through Lava Falls, taking the big hits head-on. As each person approached the rapid, tension increased and everyone was alert. As each person finished the rapid, the group grew increasingly excited with a feeling of accomplishment and pride. When we all reached Tequila Beach, freezing temperatures, high wind, and snow flurries could not cool our joy. Cold hands, wind-burned faces, numb ears were momentarily pushed from our thoughts as we celebrated good runs by finding the "mailboxes" tucked at the back of the beach, against the cliffs. We looked through the notes from other groups, drank tequila, and made our own notes to put in the box for future Grand Canyon trip groups.

Pumpkin Spring is a beautiful orange natural hot tub made of travertine that stands in contrast with the rectangular formations of limestone and basalt. As inviting as the initial scene is, the water is only luke warm, and it contains arsenic. Wading into the water, that burps up from a muddy hole, forming a disk-shaped pit of quick sand, is novel for a brief moment, and a reminder that vulcanic activity is still present (though not any immediate threat).

Pumpkin Spring made a perfect New Year's Eve campground for our trip. At mile 213, we were set for an easy float the next day, on mostly flatwater, to the next camp at mile 224. A sandy beach and terraced rocks promoted relaxed camping, and a good attitude that carried on to the next day's float, where people danced on the rafts, celebrating a good trip that was nearing its end.

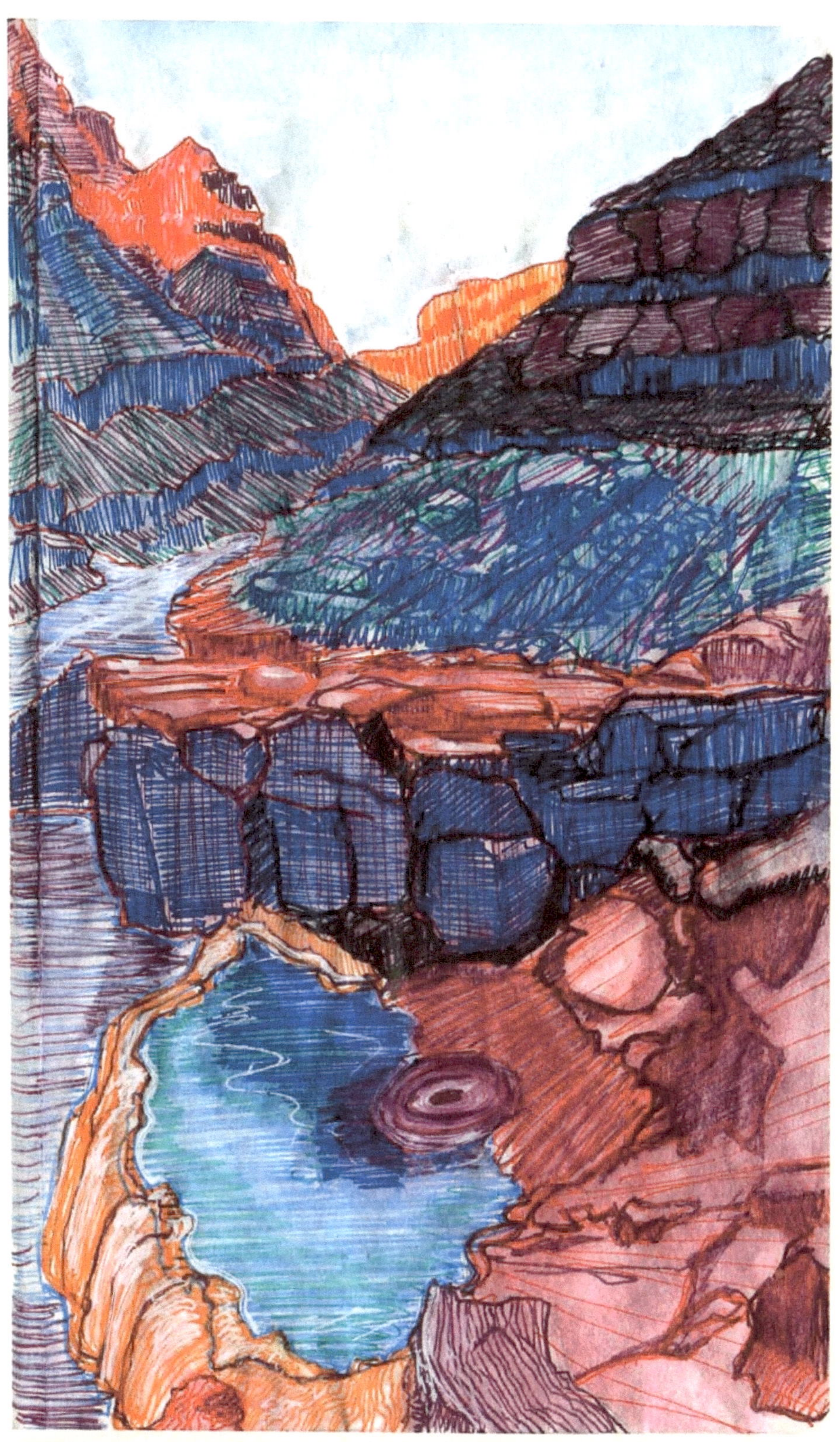

The flooding of The Nile River scared people, brought death to the unprepared, but also replenished life by depositing nutrient-rich soil along its banks. And, as the flood waters receded with perfect timing, allowing new sowing, new seeding; leaving enough water for irrigation, the valley prospered. 5000 years ago, the Egyptians understood the value of the river. The Nile gave, and the Nile took away. It was, to them, a god; a divine entity that they could not control, and could only hope to understand enough to form a cooperative relationship which would allow them to get what they must. Today, the Aswan Dam has drowned the entire Temple of Abu Simel, robs the downstream farms of annual soil nutrient replacement and forces reliance on the electricity it produces, forces the use of chemical fertilizer and allows precious water to evaporate from Lake Nasser.

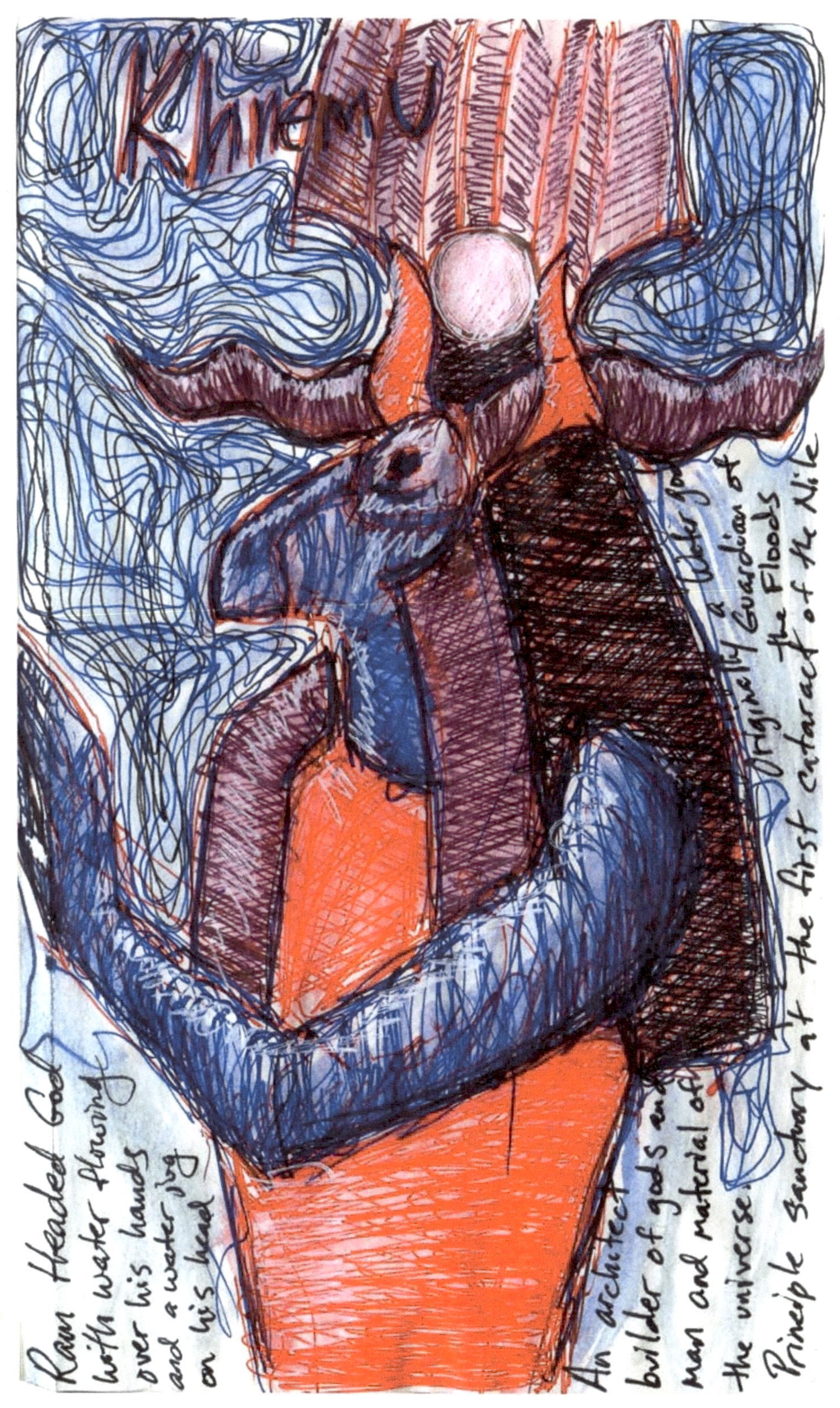
Khnemu
Ram Headed God
with water flowing
over his hands
and a water jug
on his head
An architect
builder of gods and
man and material of
the universe. Originally a water god
Guardian of the Floods
Principle Sanctuary at the first cataract of the Nile

Diamond Creek was the take out point for our trip. We knew the trip was ending when we camped in sight of Diamond Peak.

Rising from the desert floor, along the Colorado River, like an ancient pyramid, Diamond Peak is, for our trip, the end of something, and a beginning. One guide book claims that the top of the peak is at the same altitude as the man-made bridge near the put-in; Navajo Bridge. I bet that, like the pyramids of ancient Egypt, Diamond Peak will outlast the details of our own civilization

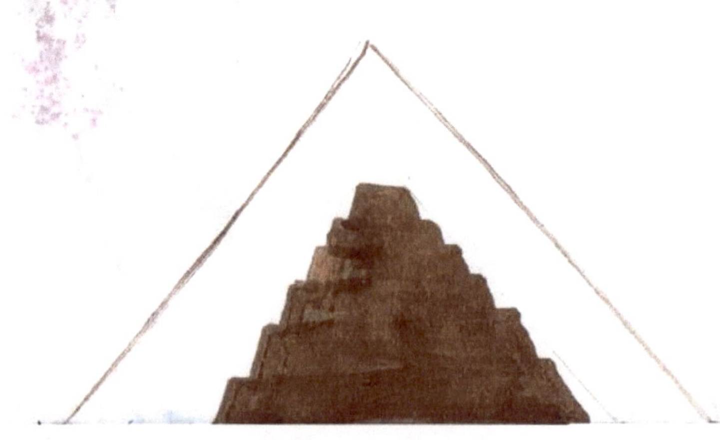

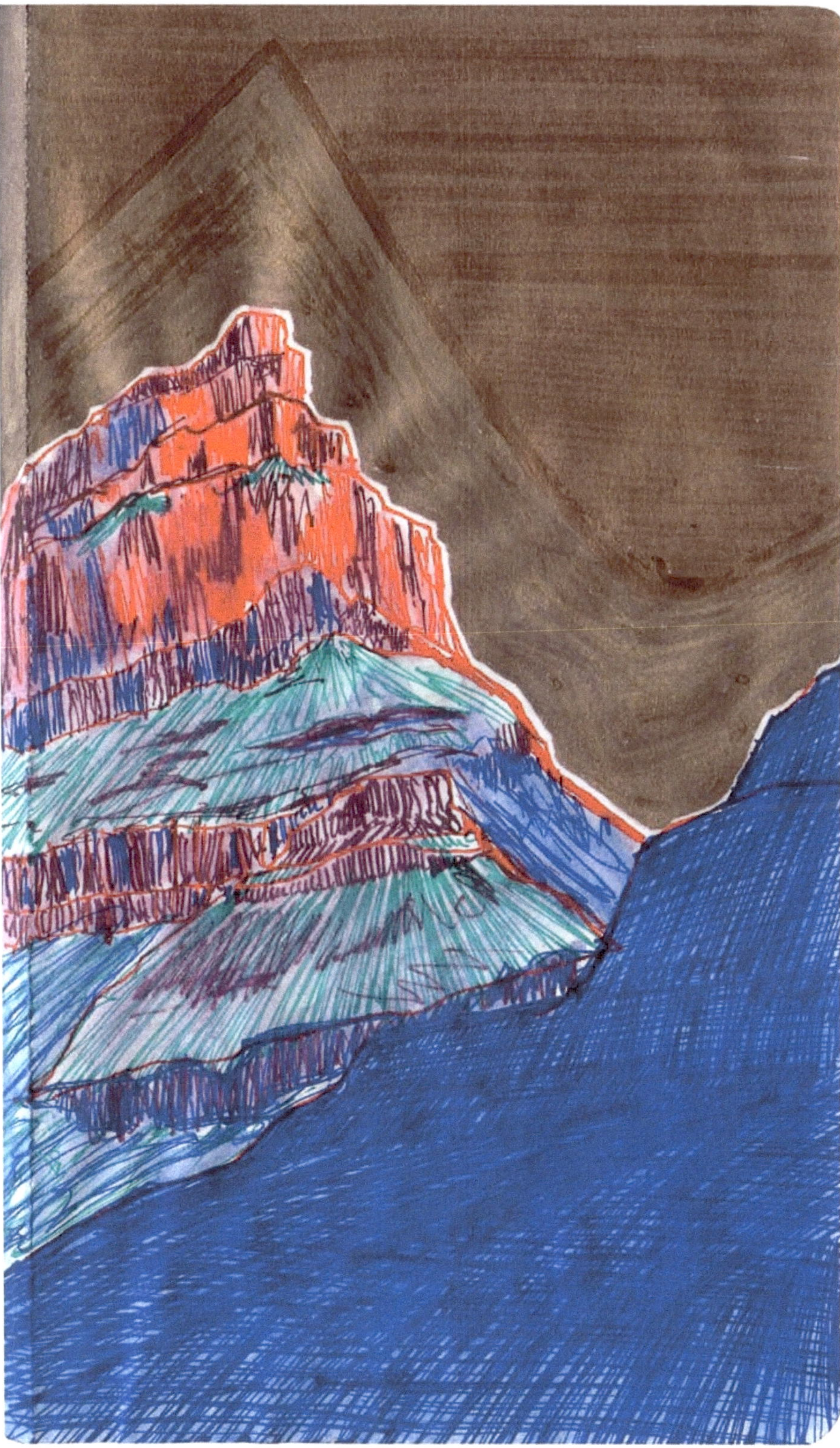

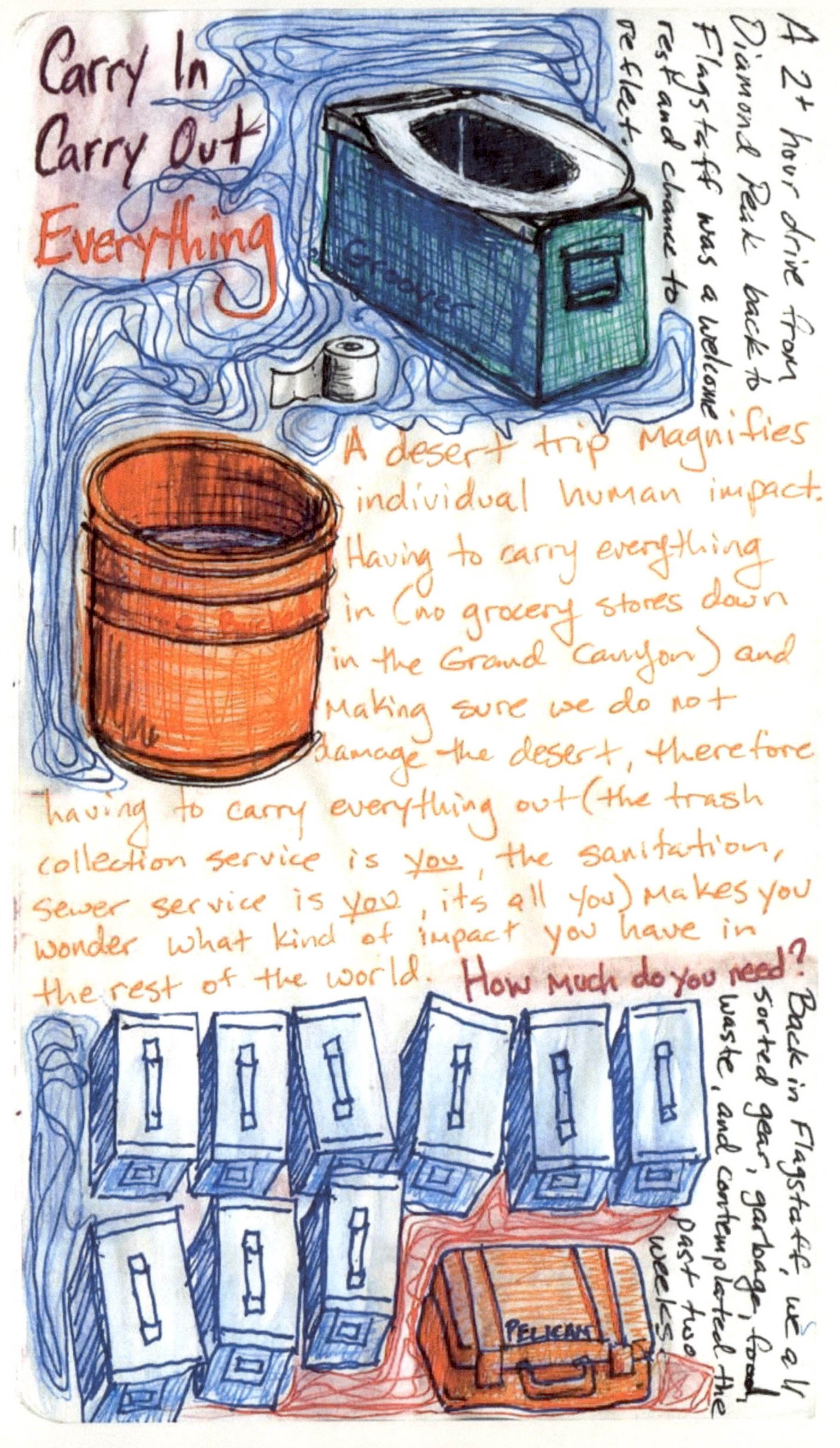
Carry In
Carry Out
Everything
A 2+ hour drive from Diamond Peak back to Flagstaff was a welcome rest and chance to reflect.
Groover
A desert trip magnifies individual human impact. Having to carry everything in (no grocery stores down in the Grand Canyon) and making sure we do not damage the desert, therefore having to carry everything out (the trash collection service is you, the sanitation, sewer service is you, it's all you) makes you wonder what kind of impact you have in the rest of the world.
How much do you need?
Back in Flagstaff, we all sorted gear, garbage, food waste, and contemplated the past two weeks.
PELICAN

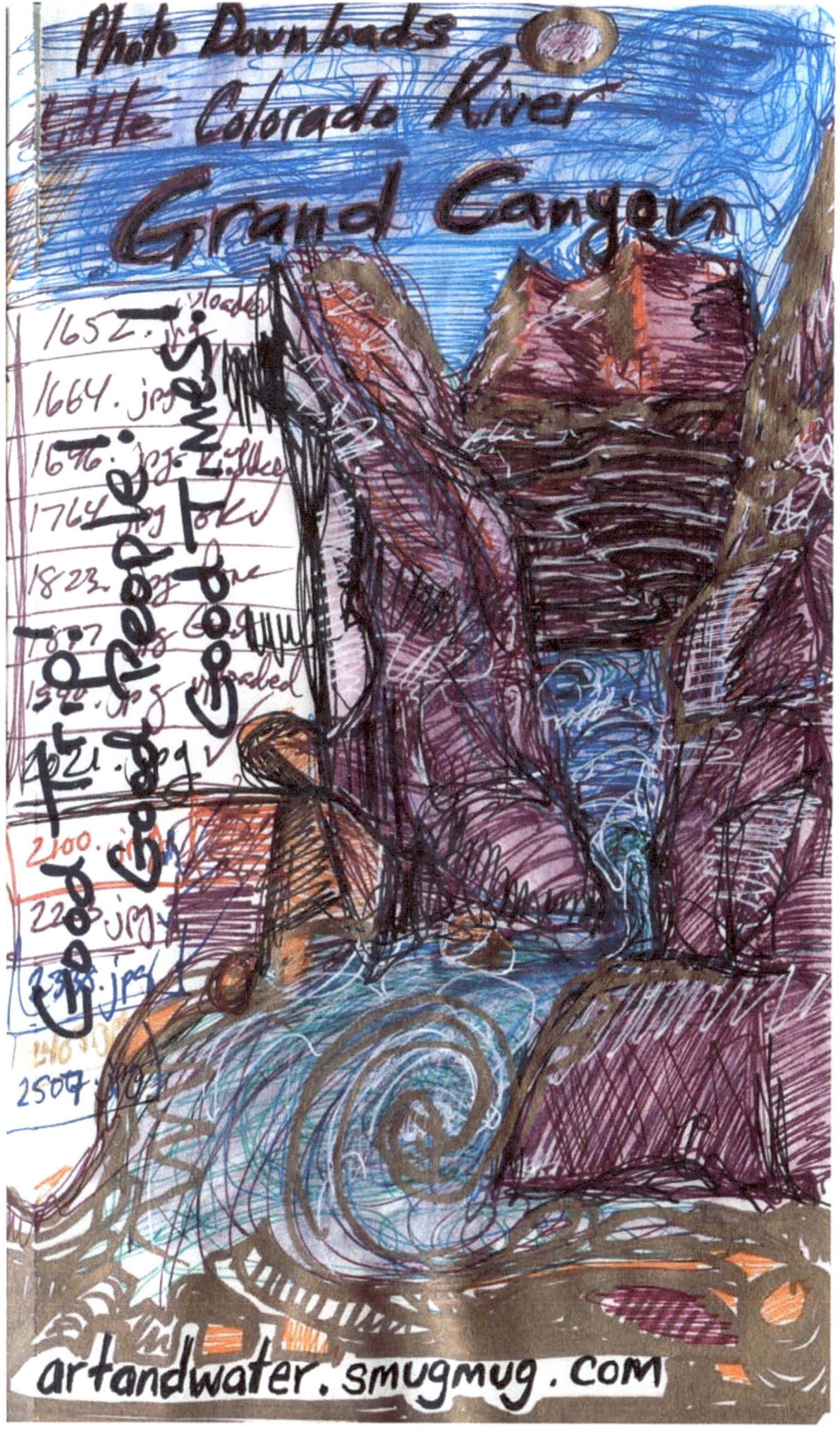
Photo Downloads
Little Colorado River
Grand Canyon
Good Trip!
Good People!
Good Times!
artandwater.smugmug.com

I WANT TO THANK THE WONDERFUL PEOPLE WHO HELPED WITH PLANNING THIS TRIP. CANYON REO, IN FLAGSTAFF, ARIZONA WAS VERY HELPFUL WITH FOOD, SHUTTLE, AND LOGISTICS. RAMSEY OUTDOOR STORE IN PARAMUS, NEW JERSEY HELPED MOST OF OUR CREW WITH PERSONAL CAMPING GEAR AND RIVER EQUIPMENT. THANKS TO SUNDOWN BAKERY IN BAYFIELD, COLORADO FOR SWEET SNACKS AND BREAD ON THE DRIVE FROM COLORADO TO ARIZONA.

THE PEOPLE WHO MADE THIS TRIP POSSIBLE, AND SHAPED IT INTO THE SUCCESS THAT IT WAS, AND DESERVE THE HIGHEST PRAISE, WERE THE PEOPLE ON THE RIVER WITH ME; "THE CREW".
MO BERGMANN, SO BERGMANN, DAN GRAYBER, GABE PORTER-HENRY, CHRISTY LIN, DAN MALTBY, KATRINA O'BRIEN, JESSICA SCHWABER, SARA WODIN-SCHWARTZ.

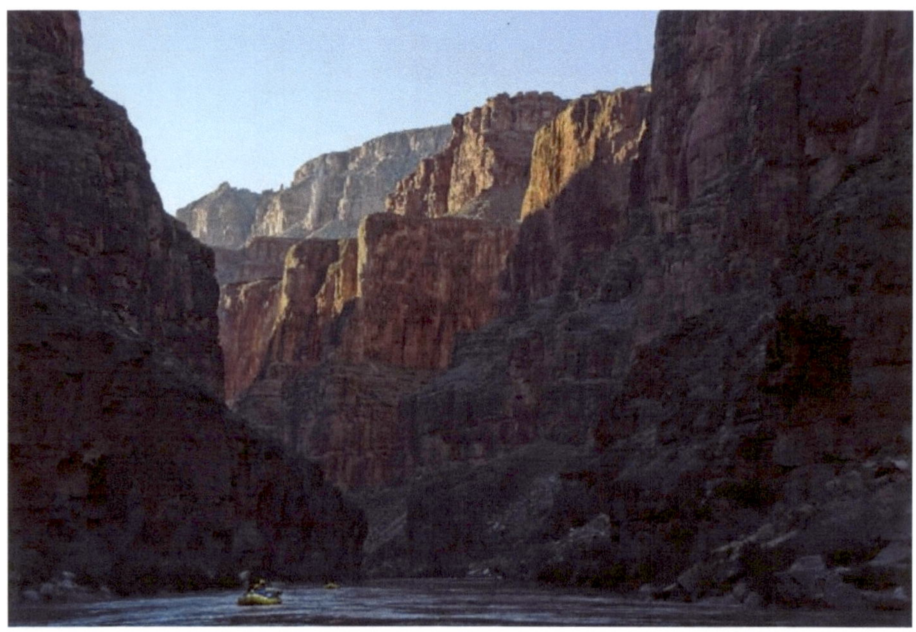

SCOTT BARNES WWW.ARTANDWATER.COM

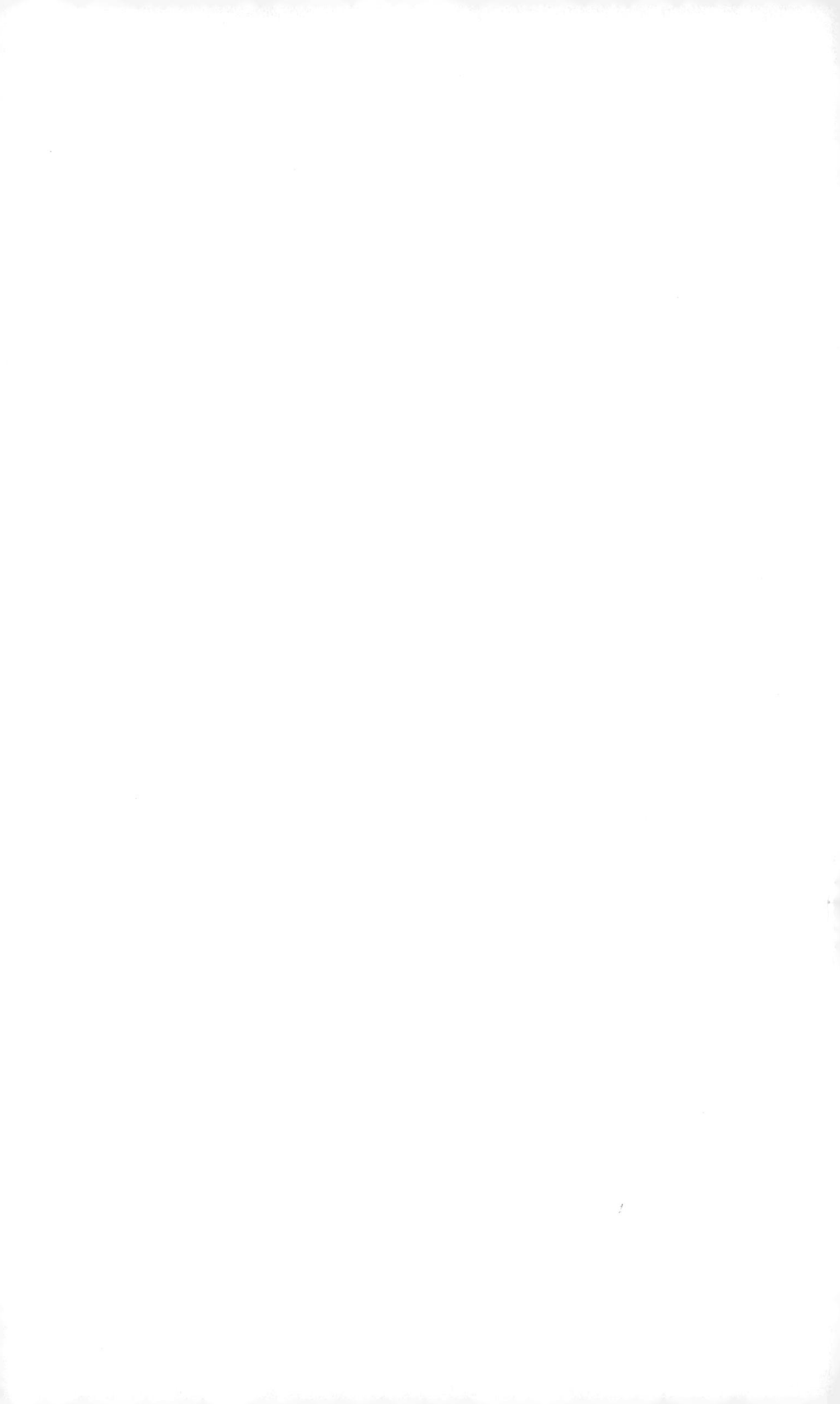

www.ingramcontent.com/pod-product-compliance
Lightning Source LLC
LaVergne TN
LVHW052300100826
845147LV00001B/101

* 9 7 8 0 6 1 5 4 4 4 0 5 5 *